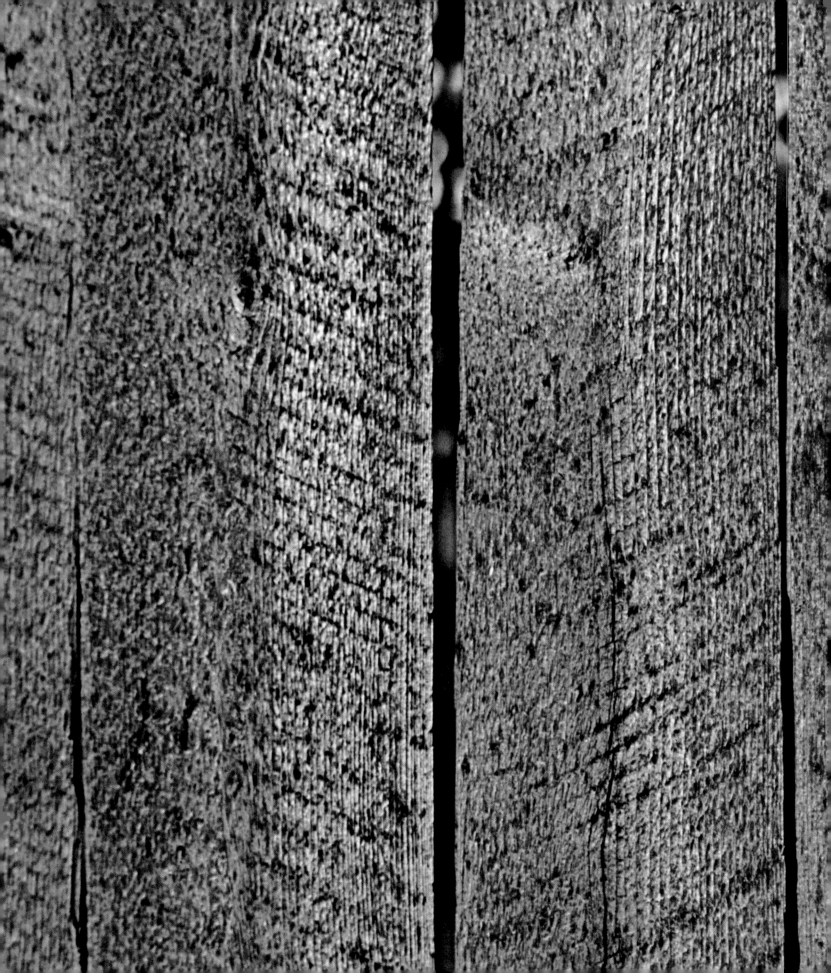

THE FAMILY CREATIVE WORKSHOP

5

Cosmetics, Costumes,
Crewelwork, Crochet, Cryptography,
Decoupage, Dioramas,
Dollhouses and Furniture,
Dolls and Doll Clothes, Dried Flowers,
Dulcimers, Egg Decorating

Plenary Publications International, Inc.
New York and Amsterdam

The Project-Evaluation Symbols appearing in the title heading at the beginning of each project have these meanings:

Range of approximate cost:

¢ Low: Under $5, or free and found natural materials

$ Medium: About $10

$$ High: Above $15

Estimated time to completion for an unskilled adult:

⊠ Hours

🕐 Days

Weeks

Suggested level of experience:

Child alone

Supervised child or family project

Unskilled adult

Specialized prior training

Tools and equipment:

Small hand tools

Large hand and household tools

Specialized or powered equipment

Publishers
Plenary Publications International, Incorporated, 300 East 40th Street, New York, 10016.

Allen Davenport Bragdon, Editor-in-Chief and Publisher of the Family Creative Workshop. President, Plenary Publications International, Inc.

Nancy Jackson, Administrative Assistant.
Jerry Curcio, Production Manager.

Editorial Preparation
Wentworth Press, Incorporated.

Walter Ian Fischman, Director.
Jacqueline Heriteau, Editor.
Francesca Morris, Executive Editor.
Susan Lusk, Art Director.
Frank Lusk, Director of Photography.
Maxine Krasnow, Production Manager.
Donal Dinwiddie, Consulting Editor.
James Wyckoff, Consulting Editor.

For this volume
Contributing editors: Lorraine Balterra, Ed Claflin, Jesárielle Damora, Nancy Deschamps, Andrea DiNoto, Jo-Anne Jarrin, Michelle Lester, Nancy Levine, William C. Mulligan, Molli Nickel, Marilyn Nierenberg, Doris Warren.

Contributing illustrators: Sonja Douglas, Fred Drucker, Jan Fairservis, Bill Hopkins, Peter Kalberkamp, Eric Koniger, Maggie MacGowan, Sally Shimizu.

Contributing photographers: Lionel Freedman, Paul Levin, Frank Lusk, Susan Lusk, Stephen McCarroll, Susan Meiselas.

Graphics and editing for Crewelwork, Cryptography, and Egg Decorating by Tree Communications, Inc., New York.

Cosmetics consultant, Helen Jane Hare, M.D. Cryptography, photo of Mary, Queen of Scots and son, James I, courtesy of the Metropolitan Museum of Art, gift of J. P. Morgan, 1917; Zimmerman Note, the National Archives; Brass Cipher disc, the National Archives. Dollhouses, antique wooden dollhouses, courtesy of the Antique Toy Department, F.A.O. Schwarz, N.Y. Dollhouse photographs on page 593, courtesy Shelburne Museum, Inc., Shelburne, Vt. Dried Flowers, contemporary style arrangements by Mrs. Myles H. Reynolds.

On the cover
Enlarged close-up of single crochet pattern in rose, pink and white. See the crochet entry, beginning on page 550. Photograph by Paul Levin.

Published by Plenary Publications International, Incorporated, 300 East 40th Street, New York, N.Y. 10016, for the Blue Mountain Crafts Council.

Library of Congress Catalog Card Number: 73–89331.
Complete set International Standard Book Number: 0–88459–021–6. Volume 5 International Standard Book Number: 0–88459–004–6.

Manufactured in the United States of America.
Printed and bound by the W. A. Krueger Company, Brookfield, Wisconsin.
Color separations by Lithotech, Incorporated, Orlando, Florida.

Contents

COSMETICS

Making Your Own Makeup

The cosmetician is often regarded as something of a sorcerer. But the truth about cosmetics, even expensive ones, is that there are few mysteries in their production. Reasonable substitutes for many products can be made safely and economically at home. As a matter of fact, some of the best cosmetics manufacturers began with just a recipe, ingredients, a large kettle, and a kitchen stove.

On the next pages are formulas for such basic cosmetic products as cold cream, vanishing cream, skin freshener, face powder and eye shadow. The chemical ingredients used are sold by chemical supply houses. You must insist that ingredients are approved by the Food and Drug Adminstration and are pure in content. One supplier catering to small mail orders is Van Waters & Rogers, P.O. Box 3200, San Francisco, California 94119. These recipes aren't made with fruits and vegetables. Recipes made with fruit and other food products do not undergo a government inspection for quality control and the possible detrimental effects are not known. These concoctions are made with ingredients that time and usage have told us are safe for all but the most unusual of skins.

Although the measurements used here have been converted from laboratory specifications into standard kitchen-utensil terms, these basic formulas are well established in the cosmetic industry. Remember as you proceed that you are following scientific formulas, not cook book recipes in which you can sometimes substitute ingredients or modify quantities. Be sure that you follow the instructions carefully, making no changes. Each formula has been tested carefully and must be followed precisely.

Try those that are most used by your family. You'll be astonished at the economies involved. As you become proficient at cooking up glamour aids, you may want to mix batches as gifts for your friends.

Marcia Donnan lives in a rustic stone cottage in the Black Hills of South Dakota with her chemist husband and two children. They have four horses, four dogs, and a cat. She has written Cosmetics from the Kitchen, *has been women's editor of the* Rapid City Journal, *and is active in state government.*

▲ Candy thermometer, pots, a kitchen range are the essential tools for making cosmetics.

◀A mortar and pestle are helpful in turning out homemade equivalents of fine cosmetic preparations (see pages 524 and 525).

Cold creams

The following five cosmetic formulas have been reviewed by Dr. Helen Hare, a prominent dermatologist in the Midwest. A fellow of the American Academy of Dermatology and certified by the American Board of Dermatology, Doctor Hare confirms that there is nothing in these recipes to cause injury to the average person using them. "They should be considered safe for general use," she says, "but if you have an unusual skin condition, consult your doctor first." The first formula is for cold cream. Study the photographs and illustrations for tips on measuring ingredients and making cosmetics.

Basic Cold Cream

½ cup mineral oil
2 tablespoons plus 1 teaspoon grated beeswax
⅔ of ¼ teaspoon borax (see photograph 3)

¼ cup plus 1 teaspoon distilled water
1 teaspoon perfume (optional)

Measure oil and beeswax as in photographs 1 and 2 in a medium-size container. Combine. Place beaker in a small, deep pot in an inch of water. Over moderate heat bring water to a boil. Lower heat to prevent burning or smoking. Stir occasionally until wax is melted. In another cup, dissolve borax in distilled water. Place the beaker in a separate pot holding about an inch of water and heat the borax solution until it just boils.

Remove from heat. Pour borax solution in a thin stream into mineral-oil mixture, stirring vigorously (see photograph 4) until temperature drops to 140F. Add perfume if desired. Continue stirring until mixture is fluffy.
Makes one cup.

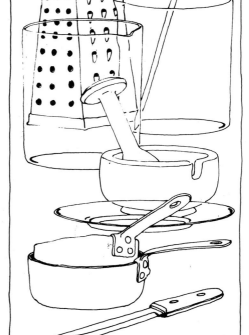

Figure A: Implements necessary to make cosmetics are found in most kitchens: spatula, or broad, flat knife; saucepan small enough to give depth and another large enough to contain small one (most double boilers have bases too broad to give depth when small quantity of ingredients are used); glass saucer or flat pane of glass for mixing powdered ingredients, as in eye shadow; mortar and pestle; glass beakers for accurate measuring, or glass measuring cups; candy thermometer; ordinary grater.

1: Measure mineral oil accurately into a measuring cup or beaker. Ratio of mineral oil to beeswax determines the consistency of the resulting products.

2: Pack grated beeswax (see figure B) as tightly as possible into the measuring spoon. Be careful not to leave air spaces between the beeswax shavings.

3: Divide ¼ teaspoon of borax powder into three equal parts on a piece of stiff paper. Combine two sections to form the required ⅔ of ¼ teaspoon measurement.

4: Use thermometer as a stirring rod when stirring emulsions. This makes it easy to keep an eye on critical temperatures as you work.

As a rule, commercial vanishing creams are light, soap-based creams made by suspending oil in water. Less oily than most cold creams, the vanishing cream below which contains no soap seems to disappear into the skin almost immediately upon application. Its moisturizing qualities are ideal for normal and oily skins. Because of its light texture, it can be used under a liquid foundation or face powder as an all-day protective base.

Basic Vanishing Cream

¼ cup plus 3 tablespoons stearic-acid powder

½ teaspoon potassium carbonate

2 tablespoons plus 2 teaspoons glycerin

1 cup plus 1 tablespoon distilled water

1 teaspoon perfume (optional)

Place stearic-acid powder in a beaker in a saucepan holding an inch of water. Heat over low fire until powdered acid liquefies. In another beaker, combine potassium carbonate, glycerin, and distilled water and heat in the same manner. When mixture reaches the boiling point, remove both saucepans with beakers from heat. Stirring constantly, pour the glycerin-water solution in a thin stream into the liquid stearic acid. Slowly stir mixture with a spatula until the carbon-dioxide bubbles stop rising. Remove beaker from pan, and with thermometer as stirring rod, continue stirring briskly until temperature of cream reaches 135F. Add perfume to strength desired, blend it well. Continue stirring until solution cools and becomes creamy. About 15 to 20 minutes. Let stand for several hours, until completely cool. Give the mixture a final stirring, and pack it into containers.

Makes 1¼ cups.

B

Figure B: To get required amount of beeswax for recipes calling for spoon measurements, rub wax on cheese grater; then press wax chips into measuring spoon.

5: Use a spatula or flat kitchen knife to pack powders like stearic acid into the appropriate measuring cup. Always make certain that your measurements are exact.

6: Use spatula to level off excess potassium carbonate from the measuring spoon back into the chemical's container. In this way, you save for your next batch.

7: Glycerin, being poured here, is an excellent emulsifying agent. It is one of the basic ingredients used to hold the cream together.

8: Use only distilled water for these formulas. Tap water risks the possibility of introducing foreign matter such as insecticides or undesirable minerals.

521

9: Stir the ingredients in both beakers until stearic-acid powder in one beaker liquefies and the glycerin solution in the other comes to a boil.

10: Use potholders, trivets, or heavy cloths to protect counter tops from the heat of saucepans and beakers just removed from boiling water.

11: Pouring one solution into another in a thin stream allows the base to absorb the new ingredients into its chemical structure.

12: Add fragrances, either pure essence or perfume, slowly, drop by drop. Use your own perfume or buy bottled essences from a chemical supply house.

13: Keep testing the final product for thickness. When the stirring rod (as shown here) or spoon is coated with a milky-white cream, the product is in its final stage.

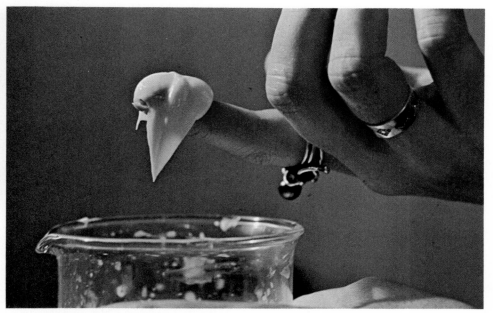

14: What looked like soapy dishwater before its 20-minute stirring becomes a rich, velvety vanishing cream. As the cream cools it also hardens but a brisk stirring before using restores the creamy consistency.

Fragrances and Distillations
Astringent

Skin fresheners—or astringents, as they are also called—are designed to fulfill several cosmetic purposes. Besides the refreshing effect they have, astringents help add life to dull-looking skin by whisking away surface dirt left by soaps or cleansing creams. Astringents are ideal for oily-skin complexions because they clear away excess skin oils: an overabundance of oil can lead to skin problems—for instance, blackheads and pimples.

The word astringent is defined as a substance that draws together or constricts tissue. This action on facial skin is quite salutary, since it brings the tissue to a healthier tone and consequently contributes to a more attractive appearance.

Although astringents generally do seem to tighten enlarged pores temporarily, no claims are made here. We do know, however, that because of the light, fresh scent included in the following recipe, this skin freshener is a stimulating pick-me-up in hot weather.

Basic Astringent

¼ teaspoon borax
3 tablespoons distilled water

2 teaspoons vodka, 40 to 60 percent alcohol
3 tablespoons rose water

Combine borax and distilled water in a beaker and place in a narrow pot holding about an inch of water. Over low heat, stir the mixture constantly until the liquid is clear and all the borax has been dissolved.

Remove beaker from heat, and let stand until the liquid is cool—this will take about 10 minutes. Now add the vodka and rose water, and stir until mixture is well blended.

Do not make any substitutions for ingredients specified.

Makes about ½ cup.

15: Combining borax and distilled water to form the liquid base of this simple-to-make skin-freshening astringent. Be absolutely certain that your measurements are precise.

▶16: Stirring the mixture over low heat until liquid becomes clear. Never leave beakers over heat unattended for even a minute. The heating progression is an integral part of the total formulation for this astringent.

17: Adding precise measurement of vodka which acts as a solvent.

18: Adding precise measure of rose water or another suitable aromatic flower water. Fragrance should be light and fresh.

Fragrances and Distillations
Powder and shadow

The preceding recipes allowed for little personal creativity, except, perhaps, the choice of fragrance. The recipes below for a loose, translucent face powder and a cream eye shadow, leave the color up to you and present a creative challenge.

The choice of shading is left up to you, with just one important stipulation: Pigments called for must be FDA-approved colorants, labeled D&C certified colorants, for use in face powders. Only inorganic colorants carrying FDA designation on the label are permitted in cosmetic preparations for use near the eye.

When adding pigments in the two following projects, be sparing at first. You can always add more. Pigments often look considerably lighter in the mortar. Upon application, however, their color may deepen two or even three

An experienced craftswoman cosmetics maker blends pigments in a well-lighted area, surrounding herself with the tools and ingredients immediately needed.

The color contrast between the actual pigment and the talc base is dramatic, but blended result will be a delicately shaded pink facial powder.

shades. And finally, remember to blend thoroughly, as shown in photographs on the opposite page, so that color is evenly distributed throughout powder or cream. Then the result will be a product with a high degree of quality.

Basic Powder

4 tablespoons talc	2 teaspoons precipitated chalk
½ teaspoon zinc oxide	½ teaspoon pigment
2 teaspoons zinc stearate	Perfume, start with ½ teaspoon

Combine all ingredients except pigment and perfume in a mortar. With pestle, rub the mixture down well until the ingredients are well blended. Then add pigment. Start with ½ teaspoon, and blend. Add more if necessary. Keep working the powder with the pestle until the mixture is evenly shaded and matches your skin. Now begin to add perfume drop by drop, blending until the consistency you like best is achieved.

Makes ⅓ cup.

Basic Eye Shadow

1 teaspoon lanolin
2 tablespoons plus 1½ teaspoons
  petrolatum (petroleum jelly)

1¼ teaspoons synthetic spermaceti wax
¼ teaspoon pigment your color choice
½ teaspoon zinc oxide

Melt first three ingredients in beaker in pan with an inch of water. Blend pigment with zinc oxide on glass plate. Add to warm base; stir. Cool until hardened. On clean glass plate, work with spatula to an even cream. Keep in air-tight container a day or two. Makes about ¼ cup.

For related projects see "Potpourris."

19: Measuring commercially prepared petroleum jelly, an ingredient that forms the base for a cream eye shadow.

20: Scraping the required amount of the petroleum jelly onto the side of the beaker is the easy way to add it.

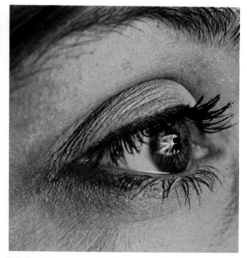

With long, even strokes, apply the cream shadow to a clean, dry lid. Be sure to blend color at the lid crease and the outer edge of the eye with your fingertip or a sponge applicator.

21: Blending eye shadow pigment with zinc oxide on a clean, flat glass surface.

22: Stirring in the pigment while the liquid base is still warm helps you to distribute the color evenly.

23: While you are blending the cooled mass on a glass plate, you may add more pigment to the cream if desired.

525

COSTUMES
From Rags To Riches

Jan Fairservis is a theater costume designer and an illustrator of books on anthropology and physiology. She illustrated Margaret Mead's People and Places *and* Costumes of the East, *written by her husband, Walter A. Fairservis. She has designed numerous costumes for theater and now designs for The Sharon Playhouse in Sharon, Conn.*

Costumes have been with mankind all through recorded history. A cave painting discovered in France shows a sorcerer in a costume of deerskin and horns; neolithic frozen graves in Siberia preserved ceremonial costumes decorated with felt and fur. Archaeologists believe religious ceremonies, tribal rituals, pageants and festivals were always conducted in appropriate costumes. Theater, which developed from ancient religious rites, has preserved the use of costumes, setting them apart from everyday clothes by exaggerations or distortions of what is familiar, by historical holdovers from former times and by exotic representations from distant lands or magical epochs.

The Magic of Costume
More popularly, costumes are associated with a foreign land or with the past, even one's own family past. Grandmother's gown can become the costume for a birthday ball or a school drama presentation. Everyday clothes are manifestations of the wearer, but when you don a costume you relinquish your own personality for the moment and accept garments appropriate to a new role. Perhaps this is why costumes have always been so compelling. They do seem to have a magical effect on the wearer as well as the observer. In a costume, you may find a new freedom.

My family loves to take part in plays, pageants, and festivals. Frequently we do not want to invest in the rental of theatrical costumes or to buy the many yards of fabric needed to make them. There is a way out of this dilemma. On the next pages are ways of making costumes of all kinds from materials that are easy to come by, and from each of the three examples, dozens of variations are possible.

Finding Raw Materials
Start by looking through thrift shops and Salvation Army stores for old evening gowns, bedspreads, curtains, draperies, and fabric remnants. Upholstery and fashion-fabric stores occasionally have sales where interesting yardage is sold at reduced prices. Attics often harbor old dresses, men's outdated formal clothes, old ballet tights, hats and gloves.

Actually, almost anything can become a costume or an accessory to a costume. Brown paper bags can be recycled into Halloween goblin costumes or cowboy-and-Indian outfits as shown on pages 528 and 529. Sheets and old bedspreads can be converted into draped costumes from classical lands, as on page 530. Old clothing from the past (page 532) is easy to recycle into great costumes for a play, a party or some other special event. From the principle of the one-dress pattern (page 533) you can make all kinds of costumes. The caftan, page 534, can be a starting point for many variations, as can any of the period costumes on page 535.

Make-Up and Make Believe
But your "costume" does not end with the clothing. Hair style, hair cut, wigs, beards, and mustaches are essential parts of the total effect you are considering. And so, of course, is make-up. The make-up section on pages 536 and 537 describes some of the basics of theatrical make-up and the type of symbolic make-up used by clowns and dancers.

Starting with the examples of costume and make-up shown here, you can develop all kinds of marvelous creations.

Teviot Fairservis, Jan's 19-year-old daughter, wears a Restoration costume made from two thrift shop evening dresses. Panniers that spread the skirt are described on page 532.

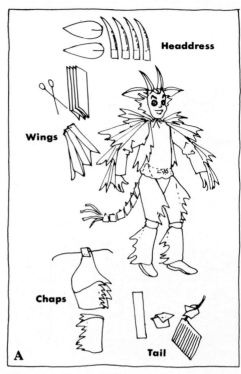

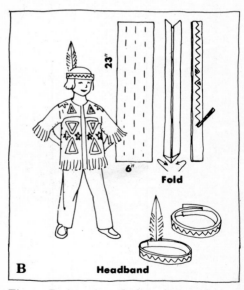

Paper Folding and Cutting
Paper costumes

With paper, scissors, a stapler, masking tape, string, and cardboard, wild headdresses and costumes can be made. My daughter, Beth, was a goblin in a costume made from eight paper bags. Headdress with cardboard horns and ears taped together, has paper sideburns. Wings were pleated, cut, spread, and stapled to the paper sleeves. Chaps, attached to a string belt, were in two pieces so Beth could run. Tail started with a paper tassel; then links of cut paper were twisted and stapled up the string. Wings were tied on with string across the shoulders, and a matching sweater hid most of the strings. Making the jacket on the opposite page is a simple project a child can share.

Figure A: This goblin costume is made of paper bags. The jagged cutting on the edges of each part and the pleated wings give it a weird, devilish look.

Figure B: American Indian designs look good on buckskin-colored (grocery bag) paper. Headband is folded into strips as shown, decorated, then stapled or glued.

Beth's goblin costume was not cut to a precise pattern. The pieces were cut and stapled together to fit her. Strings secure horns, sleeves, chaps, and tail.

Children have fun making and decorating a paper-bag jacket like the one at right.

1: Cut bottoms off two paper bags. Cut bags open at the seam. Fold one bag in half lengthwise for yoke and sleeve piece. Cut other bag in half vertically to form back. Cut other half in half again vertically to form the two front pieces.

2: Cut semicircle to fit neck at center of yoke fold. Cut V-shaped front opening.

There is enough paper in only two large grocery bags to make a jacket of Indian (or other) design for a seven-year-old. Use big scissors to cut the bags, following the photographs on this page. It's easier if you work on a large area, like the floor. After you have cut the bags you can staple them together in a matter of minutes. I like a hand-held stapler, but a table type can be used. For decorating, the colors of crayons, felt-tip pens or poster paints show up well on this paper. Indian or peasant motifs or abstract designs created by the child hold special appeal.

3: After placing a front piece on yoke front at opening, attach top of front to bottom of yoke with staples, 3 inches apart, forming ½-inch seam. Repeat.

4: Staple bottom of sleeves after fronts are folded down and seams flattened. Omit underarm staples. Attach back in same manner. Staple front pieces to the back.

You may want to outline coloring areas on the first jacket you and your child make, to teach a traditional design. The author did these scallops and flowers.

5: Tie a string securely around the waist to take some of the fabric's weight from shoulders and to hold the folds in place.

Needlecrafts
Drapes and wraparounds

Collect discarded bedspreads, sheets, draperies, and curtains to make impressive draped costumes that look as if they came from ancient classical lands. Use ribbon, chain or string, heavy safety pins, or brooches to hold the draped fabric. Making folds with pleasing lines and balancing the fabric's weight on the shoulders are objectives of good draping. Two or three pieces of fabric may be needed to make a costume. The top sketches in figure C show how the right arm is left free. A wraparound costume must be of light, soft material. The one at the bottom of figure C is from the design of an Egyptian dress. Several pins are needed to keep a draped or wrapped costume secure when the wearer moves about.

Figure C: With large pieces of fabric, you can drape capes and garments like these.

The line of a draped costume based on ancient models has grace and beauty.

Needlecrafts
Circular patterns

One of the most valuable tricks in costume making is to know how to make arcs and circles. With circular patterns, and the figures below, you can make capes, skirts, sleeves, headdress and crown. To use a string as a compass, first smooth the material on a large, flat surface. Place a tack in the center of the proposed circle. Tie a string around it and tie a piece of chalk or a pencil or marker on the other end. Holding the string tight, draw your circle or arc.

The folds and the movement of a full cape make it very theatrical. This cape has a wide cuff of brocade to resemble an ancient bishop's vestment.

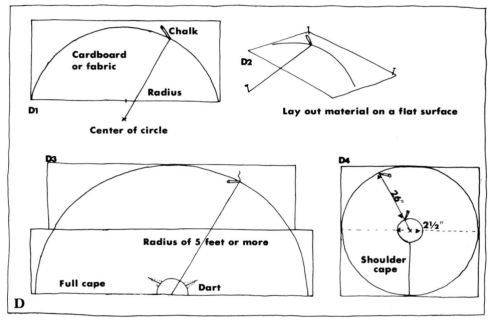

Figure D: D1 and D2 show drawing semi-circular patterns. Figure D3 shows pieced fabric being measured for a full cape. D4 shows measurements for a shoulder cape.

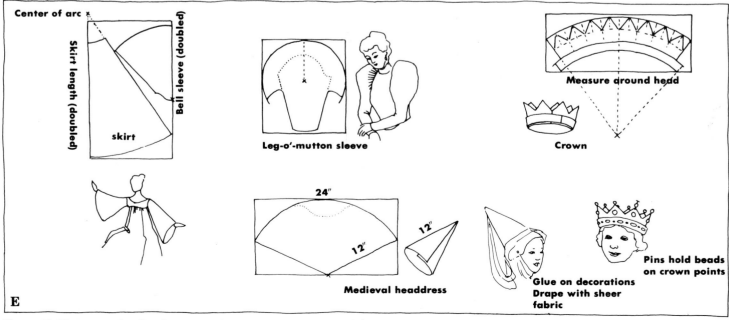

Figure E: These are details of patterns for sleeves, skirt (which fold double), crown, headdress. Measure length of skirt and of arm.

1840

conservative
1840–1900

1890's
dandy

Puritan

F

Needlecrafts
Thrift-shop finds

The basic shape of men's clothes has not changed so very much in the past century. Most of the changes have been in details—buttons, cuffs, lapels, jacket lengths, pocket flaps, and shoulder lines. Women's clothes have varied more radically, but the Restoration costume on page 527 is an illustration of what can be done with an old evening dress. Such historic costumes depend on underskirt supports.

Dressing Up for 1840
In the early 1800s a man was expected to wear a wide, colorful scarf, or a stock, and a very high collar. This romantic style of dress was adopted by English gentlemen as well as dandies, and was eventually accepted everywhere in Europe and America. Later on, during the Victorian age, men began to wear collars and ties similar to those used today.

The costume (figure F) of a young man of the 1840s consists of a jacket from a 1950s natural-shoulder suit of beige gabardine. Darts added front and back shaped a low, tight waistline. The pants were decuffed and narrowed, then steam ironed without a crease. Straps that go under the shoes hold the trouser legs at the instep. The collar was covered with velveteen. The waistcoat is plaid taffeta salvaged from an old evening dress. The tie is black silk. A girl's broad-brimmed, natural-straw hat with a black ribbon makes an acceptable hat.

◄Figure F: Thrift-shop men's suits are the basis for these period costumes. Pants may be narrowed or cut off, lapels reset, buttons changed to alter the style. The text describes how some of these costumes were made.

►Figure G: Panniers for the Restoration costume pictured on page 527 are made of paper bags stuffed with newspaper and stapled to a tape around the waist. A bustle at the back or a farthingale that encircles the hips under the skirt can be made this way instead of using devices of wire and tape.

G

A Somber Suit for 1620
The Puritans, 1620 to 1700, were poorly dressed compared with the Colonists in southern towns and New York. Because of their religious beliefs, the Puritans avoided gaudy elaborate dress, wearing costumes that had somber colors and simple lines. The Puritan costume can be copied by using a 1940s suit with wide leg pants and a long jacket, still available second-hand. This suit was a gray wool sharkskin with some of the effect of hand-woven fabric. New darts front and back made the jacket fit close to the chest and appear high-waisted. Shoulder seams were slit, and a fold of fabric replaced the pads and stood out, as in the Colonial period. Large snaps and eight to ten buttons up the front, wide white collar and deep cuffs gave the jacket an authentic look. The pants were cut off two inches below the knee. Heavy matching ribbon, long enough to be tied at the side, was sewed to each pant leg. Lines of buttons up the sides added another authentic touch. Gray knee socks, black shoes, and a Boy Scout ranger style hat, sprayed black, finished this costume.

Needlecrafts
Basic one-dress pattern

Making costumes for children or adults to wear in a play or a pageant, or to a fancy-dress party, is a pleasant kind of sewing because the garments do not need finely finished details—the costume's line is the most important thing to achieve. It takes much less time if you work with a basic dress or dress pattern that fits the person. Besides, an impatient subject usually will not stand still long enough for you to cut and fit a muslin pattern. Start with a simple classic dress, robe, or suit, and modify it to look like a picture of the costumed character. Figure H shows how a basic dress for a little girl can be varied.

The basic-dress pattern (figure H) had puff sleeves and a long skirt cut in four pieces. This was particularly adaptable because it didn't have a seam up the front. The dress could be belted very high with a ribbon to make a Kate Greenaway or an Empire costume.

Dressing a Princess, Peasant and Queen

To make a Renaissance costume for a little princess—the Snow White dress—the bodice fullness was stitched to a stiffened underbodice. A curved belt gave the deep, pointed bodice line needed; the belt was cut from cardboard and covered with fabric. The ruff was made of three circles of organdy (center circle 1-inch radius, large circle 8-inch radius) slit on the straight of the material, and the three were sewed together. Then they were pleated like a fan and sewed to a ribbon, which anchored the ruff to the dress and protected the back of the neck. The skirt was lifted away from the hips by a farthingale, made of small paper bags as seen in figure G. Long, narrow sleeves were added.

The basic dress became a peasant costume for an operetta with the addition of embroidered tape. A great variety of embroidered ribbons and tapes is available in fabric stores because these decorations have become so fashionable. The tape was sewed around the neckline and as cuffs on the puff sleeves. You can trim the apron with it, or perhaps sew several narrow bands on a shorter skirt to go over the basic dress. This overskirt should be a bright, plain color. If you are making many peasant outfits, fancy tapes might be too expensive; bias strips of patterned cloth could be used instead. The once-popular lace-trimmed crinolines have been preserved in many attics; one of these can add fullness and bounce to the skirt. Fitted boots are handsome with a peasant costume; but tights and ballet shoes are good, too.

The medieval costume for a girl playing a queen in a fairy tale is worn over a contrasting-color turtleneck knit shirt. The sash, almost three yards long, was made of silky brocade. The headdress was made in three layers. First, a bright silk kerchief, covering part of the forehead, was tied around the head. Then a white wimple was wound under the chin and secured on top of the head. Finally, a light silk veil, long enough to hang to the hips, was pinned on top, to float behind the wearer. A small crown was cut from cardboard, using the arc pattern (figure E, page 531), shellacked, and painted gold.

Boned undergarments, hoops or wire frameworks, and many petticoats added to the weight and grandeur of women's clothing until the age of central heating and liberation began in this century. Even children in advanced European countries were confined in tight-fitting bodices and ornate clothing. Today, our children enjoy dressing up in long skirts and big hats, and little girls imitate tight bodices by cinching belts around their waists. Adults have exclaimed over the feeling of elegance given them by the costumes they have worn—high, stiff collars, ruffles and lace, great capes, heavy clothing made of rich fabrics. With a basic knowledge of machine sewing and a pattern as a starting point, you can produce costumes for all occasions that will be worn with great delight.

Basic dress pattern

Renaissance princess

Peasant girl

Medieval queen

H

Figure H: The basic dress was found in an easy-to-sew section of a pattern book. Detail sketches show how belt and ruff were cut for dress adapted for a Renaissance princess; the peasant and the fairy tale queen costumes are also from the same dress.

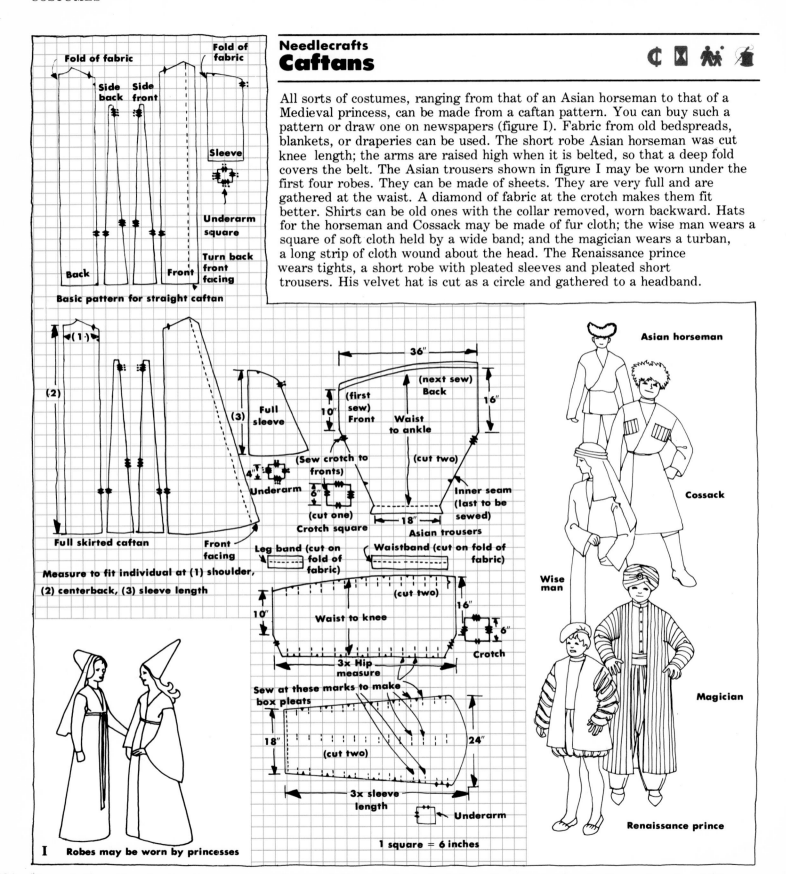

Needlecrafts
Caftans

All sorts of costumes, ranging from that of an Asian horseman to that of a Medieval princess, can be made from a caftan pattern. You can buy such a pattern or draw one on newspapers (figure I). Fabric from old bedspreads, blankets, or draperies can be used. The short robe Asian horseman was cut knee length; the arms are raised high when it is belted, so that a deep fold covers the belt. The Asian trousers shown in figure I may be worn under the first four robes. They can be made of sheets. They are very full and are gathered at the waist. A diamond of fabric at the crotch makes them fit better. Shirts can be old ones with the collar removed, worn backward. Hats for the horseman and Cossack may be made of fur cloth; the wise man wears a square of soft cloth held by a wide band; and the magician wears a turban, a long strip of cloth wound about the head. The Renaissance prince wears tights, a short robe with pleated sleeves and pleated short trousers. His velvet hat is cut as a circle and gathered to a headband.

Fold of fabric
Fold of fabric

Side back **Side front**

Sleeve

Underarm square

Turn back front facing

Back **Front**

Basic pattern for straight caftan

Full skirted caftan

Front facing

Measure to fit individual at (1) shoulder,
(2) centerback, (3) sleeve length

Full sleeve

Underarm

Crotch square

(Sew crotch to fronts)

(cut one)

36"

(next sew) **Back**

(first sew) **Front**

Waist to ankle

16"

(cut two)

Inner seam (last to be sewed)

18"

Asian trousers

Leg band (cut on fold of fabric)

Waistband (cut on fold of fabric)

(cut two)

16"

Waist to knee

6"

Crotch

3x Hip measure

Sew at these marks to make box pleats

18"

(cut two)

24"

3x sleeve length

Underarm

1 square = 6 inches

Asian horseman

Cossack

Wise man

Magician

Renaissance prince

I **Robes may be worn by princesses**

Figure I: From these basic patterns many costume variations can be devised, depending on your imagination and sewing ability.

Needlecrafts
Making a period dress

From any period dress pattern of the type found in most pattern books you can make costumes ranging from the seventeenth to the twentieth century. Adjustments are made in the fit of the bodice, the slope of the shoulder seam, and the way sleeves fit into the armholes. The costumes shown in figure J are simplified, and bodice and skirt are sewed together. The bodice must be lined with strong fabric; boning, often used in evening dresses, is sewed on at the darts front and back. A long zipper up the back makes putting on the bodice quick and easy. Heavy-duty snaps keep strain off the zipper, hold the fold of cloth that hides it and fasten up the back of the skirt.

Figure J shows the decorations characteristic of dresses worn at the dates noted. The 1640 dress has a fan collar (see figure H, page 533), a fabric-covered cardboard triangle in front and added puff sleeves. The 1680 dress needs the collar in the drawing. The 1780 dress is trimmed with box-pleated, 4-inch-wide strips. The high 1830 waistline makes boning unnecessary, but

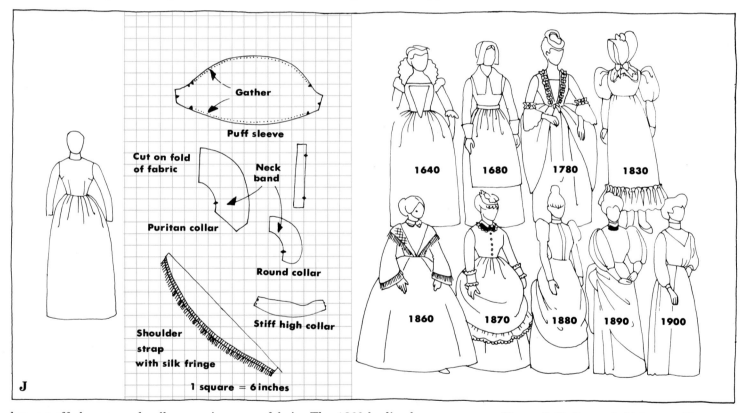

large puff sleeves and collar require more fabric. The 1860 bodice has shoulder straps and bell sleeves (see figure E, page 531). The 1880 dress has leg-o'-mutton sleeves, also in figure E. The puff sleeves of 1890 are huge and come below the elbow.

Skirts change the line of a costume radically, but are not as hard to make as bodices. They should be at least 5 yards around the hem, except for the 1830 dress, for which 3 yards will do. The pleated ruffle, however, requires quite a bit of fabric. Although all the skirts are cut in four gores, the angle of the gores varies, because some skirts are gathered at the waist. Dresses of 1780, 1870, 1880, and 1890 have two skirts, draped over a farthingale or bustle, and extra length must be allowed for that.

A skirt is draped by pinning it to a tape around the waist of a model wearing a bustle and petticoat. It is then sewed and attached to the bodice.

Figure J: Bodice and skirt proportions and decorative details differ, but simplified costumes of all these styles from 1640 to 1900 may be built on a basic-dress pattern.

How to make up

Joseph Bednerz is a freelance hair stylist and make-up artist for fashion and beauty magazines. He is the personal stylist for a number of theatrical, business and political personalities.

A make-up artist uses a person's face as a painter uses a canvas—as the base for a painting. In the instance of the make-up artist, colors are used to create an illusion based on the subject's features, an illusion that lasts only a short while. Like the painter's art, that of the make-up artist has lately "gone public." That is to say, materials that were once available only to professional make-up artists can now be found at many cosmetic counters. Everyone is doing it with make-up, just as it seems "everyone" is painting, at least on Sunday.

While small quantities of make-up can be purchased anywhere, large quantities to be used in shows and colors needed for special theatrical effects may be ordered from mail-order houses such as Paramount Theatrical Supplies, 32 West 20th Street, New York, N.Y. 10011, and Irving's Theatrical Make-up Service, 305 East Ridgewood Avenue, Ridgewood, N.J. Manufacturers make tubes of base color in a wide variety of skin tones; clown white and many colors for liner and shading come in small pots. Also available are a powder used to keep make-up from smudging, powder puffs, and soft brushes to remove excess powder.

The masklike make-up in three colors in figure K shows some of the basic make-up principles, with the features symbolized as nice, happy, weird, and evil. These examples—the faces of two dancers, a clown, and an actor—were chosen because they are so simplified.

The first step in applying make-up is to blank out all features, including eyebrows and lips, with the base color. Base is dabbed on in spots all over the face and neck, then blended with the fingertips to a thin, even coating. Symbolic make-up is painted over this without regard for the real features.

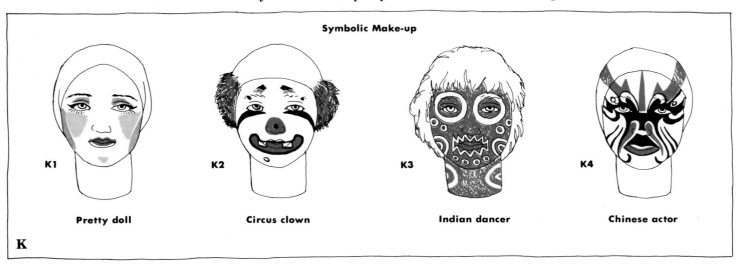

Symbolic Make-up

K1 — Pretty doll

K2 — Circus clown

K3 — Indian dancer

K4 — Chinese actor

K

Figure K1: Clown-white base. Blend gray on lids, pink on cheeks and chin, black to outline eyes and above brow line, draw low lashes, curved red lips. K2: Clown-white base. Outline smiling mouth and teeth on chin; red mouth, nose and spots on cheeks; black areas on eyes painted in. K3: Thin clown-white base. Outline areas that are white here with brown pencil; fill in the rest with red. K4: Clown-white base, pencil outline areas; fill in with white, black to outline eyes, and red at lips, painted on with soft brushes. Use your imagination to create similar masks, drawn and colored on clown-white base.

Character make-up is based on the existing features of the subject. The make-up begins with the application of a flesh-color base chosen to indicate youthful or aged skin, or skin of a particular type. To raise features or to fill hollows, shade base with a lighter color; to deepen hollows or level raised features, shade base with a darker color. A good way to study the fundamentals of this shading technique is to work on an aging make-up, as shown on the next page. To create a character face, highlight the real features' raised areas—nose, cheekbones, for instance, and darken existing hollows. To make wrinkles, paint on, then blend, dark lines in the tiny shadows and creases of the skin. See figure L.

For related projects and entries, see "Cosmetics," "Masks," "Marionettes," "Pageants and Parades," "Puppets," and "Sewing."

The make-up table is covered with containers of color in various forms.

The back of a make-up artist's hand is his palette. Liner can be warmed and blended there with a soft brush.

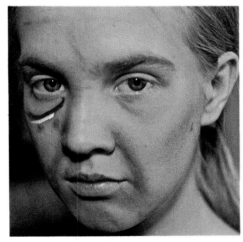

Two views of Tevy wearing aging makeup. The clearly marked lines, left view, have been blended into the base makeup on the right side. Tevy's existing features have been used as the point of departure for coloring that darkens hollows, lightens raised areas. Black line under the eye becomes a wide shadow when blended, and the white line below it raises Tevy's high cheekbones, emphasizing the hollow.

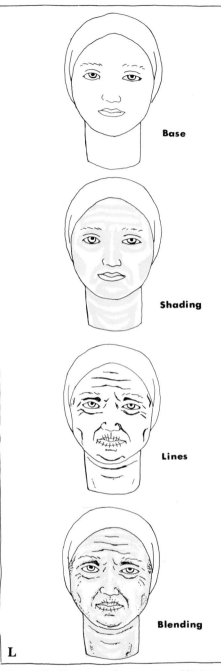

Base

Shading

Lines

Blending

L

Figure L: Sketches show areas of light and shadow to be accented and lines to be drawn in creases and frown marks. They create the illusion of a face worn by time and emotion. The character qualities of good or evil will show in the wrinkles formed by years of kindly smiles or of frowning and sneering. Creating this face is an art, but it can be learned.

The series of pictures at right shows the application of subtle make-up for photography. Less subtle make-up is used for stage; the lines are not blended, but the hard edge on one side is removed with the side of the thumb.

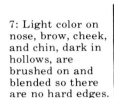

6: Base is dabbed on with fingers or applied in spots over all the face and neck. Then it is blended to cover evenly.

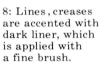

7: Light color on nose, brow, cheek, and chin, dark in hollows, are brushed on and blended so there are no hard edges.

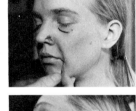

8: Lines, creases are accented with dark liner, which is applied with a fine brush.

9: Light and dark accent creases in the neck.

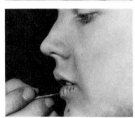

10: Fine lines of age cross the lips to break the soft outline of a young mouth.

11: Powder is put on the surface of make-up to keep it from smudging. Excess powder is brushed away.

12: Finally, hair is powdered to take away brightness, and the make-up is completed.

Magic with Stitchery

*Mildred J. Davis is an internationally known author (*The Art of Crewel Embroidery, Early American Embroidery Designs*), lecturer, teacher, and research authority on textiles. She is Consulting Curator of the Textile Resource and Research Center, Valentine Museum, Richmond, Va., where she organizes and directs its Assemblies for Embroiderers. Most recently she conducted its first International Assembly at Sea. She lives in Chestnut Hill, Mass.*

Crewel embroidery is one of the most ancient forms of embroidery, dating back to the fifth-century A.D. in Egypt. A colorful and demanding needlecraft, it derives its name from the use of a special crewel yarn. This is a fine wool yarn with a slight sheen that usually comes in the form of two plies tightly twisted together to form a single strand. A strand can be used singly for delicate effects or many strands can be combined for bolder designs. Traditionally, embroidery is not considered to be crewelwork if worked in a different yarn. There is a durable quality to crewels and they have been widely used for household and personal accessories; coverlets, curtains, clothing, chair seats, cushions, and rugs may be worked in this medium.

None of the stitches used in crewel embroidery are exclusively "crewel" stitches, so the beginning embroiderer will discover it is easy to go on to other techniques, using these stitches as the starting point. In addition, the nature of crewel embroidery allows for individual interpretation, whether the design is completely original or not.

The sampler opposite is my interpretation of a traditional design that provides a good introduction to crewelwork. This sampler includes 36 of the embroidery stitches typically found in contemporary American crewelwork.

Needlecrafts
Crewel embroidery sampler

Materials
Background fabrics: The sampler was worked on linen twill with single 2-ply strands of crewel yarn. Traditionally, crewel is worked on linen, linen twill, cotton and linen woven together, wool, or silk. Today, we also use handwoven linen, silk, denim, and textured fabrics, including synthetics and burlap. The durable, firm weave of linen and silk anchors the stitches while permitting easy passage for the needle and thread.

Yarns: The crewel yarns (sometimes called threads) used in the sampler can be found in beautiful gradations of color. Made by American as well as European firms, they vary in weight, size, twist, and appearance. Synthetic yarns with many of the qualities of crewel wool yarns are available. In general, choose a yarn according to the fabric you are using. Loosely woven, coarse fabrics are usually worked with two or three strands of wool used simultaneously. Tightly woven, fine fabrics usually call for a single strand. Try sample stitches on the fabric for a crewelwork piece to judge the number of strands to use.

Needles: The sampler was worked with a No. 22 chenille needle. Selection of the proper needle is important. Needle sizes must be correlated to fabric weave and yarn. The needle must be slightly larger than the yarn to permit the yarn to go through the fabric without fraying. Crewel and chenille needles, both pointed, are used for crewelwork. Crewel needles, sold in sizes 1 to 10, are about 1¾ inches long, with an easy-to-thread ⅛-inch eye. Popular sizes are 3, 4, and 5 (the smallest of the three sizes). Chenille needles are about 1½ inches long, with a ¼-inch eye. Popular sizes are 20, 22, and 24 (the smallest). When working stitches such as the Whipped or Woven Spider Web (page 543), use a tapestry needle. The blunt end will not pick up the fabric or split your threads.

This enlarged photograph shows a crewelwork sampler designed by Mildred Davis. The traditional motifs are done in muted tones of crewel yarn on linen twill. Instructions for the 36 embroidery stitches used here are given on pages 542-545.

EMBROIDERY CRAFTNOTES: PREPARATION AND TECHNIQUES

Threading the needle and handling yarn lengths

Cut yarn 18 to 24 inches long; a longer strand might fray by the time you reach its end. To thread the yarn: Fold back a few inches of yarn at one end of strand to make a loop.

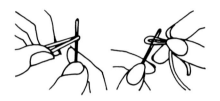

Pull loop taut around the head of the needle (above, left), and pinch this fold with thumb and forefinger. Slip loop off needle and push the pinched fold through the eye of the needle (above, right).

Starting and finishing yarn

When starting a length of yarn, knot the end and insert the needle in the fabric so the knot lies on the wrong side. When you reach the end of a yarn length, weave the thread under a few stitches on the wrong side, and clip the end close to the fabric. Begin subsequent new threads by weaving them under the nearest few stitches on the wrong side.

Working with a hoop

Each time the needle is inserted, it goes in vertically with a jabbing motion. Keep one hand above the standing floor hoop and the other below it, as shown in the drawing.

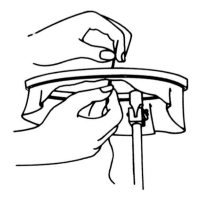

Other accessories: A small, sharp pair of embroidery scissors; a thimble; and an embroidery frame or hoop. Hoops, which are sold in many sizes and styles, such as hand-held or standing floor hoops, stretch the fabric and help you make uniform, unpuckered stitches.

Methods

Transferring the pattern: The first step in making the sampler is to transfer the embroidery pattern to the background material. You will need tracing paper; dressmaker's carbon paper; soft and hard lead pencils; straight pins; and a piece of sturdy, flat-surfaced fabric measuring at least 13-by-11½ inches (to allow a 2-inch margin on all sides for blocking—the shaping process—and framing). I used a linen twill, but a round-thread, Belgian, or Irish linen may be substituted. Place a sheet of tracing paper over the actual size pattern on the opposite page. With a soft pencil, trace the design, omitting numbers and names. Place the linen, right side up, on a table; center the tracing, penciled side up, over it. Pin paper to fabric margins with pins pointing outward; pin around three sides only, leaving one side open. Insert the carbon paper, carbon side down, between tracing paper and fabric. With a dull, hard lead pencil, trace the entire design onto the fabric; lift up the open side occasionally, to see how well the carbon is transferring. Remove pins and papers.

Making the sampler: The sampler pattern opposite has two main elements: a border of blocks of embroidery stitches, and a central motif using most of the stitches employed in the border blocks. It is a good idea to work the border blocks first, to become familiar with the stitches, before you undertake the central motif. The directions for the sampler border are given on pages 546–549, and are divided into two sections. Pages 546 and 547 describe the making of the top portion of the border; pages 548 and 549, the bottom. Each block within the border is shown enlarged for clarity and is described in detail with a key to the names on the pattern on the opposite page. The numbers in the text refer to the corresponding numbers used in the sequential stitch instructions (pages 542–545).

The large central motif includes most of the stitches used in the border blocks. The stitches for this section are identified by their sequential numbers on the pattern on the opposite page; use the picture on page 539 as a guide for color. Begin the central motif by working the easiest stitches first, those lowest in the numerical sequence, and then progress to the more difficult stitches.

Colors are indicated in the text, but if you wish to change the color scheme of the sampler, choose yarn in a color suited to your decor, and with four or five color gradations available. Do not hesitate to experiment with color, but do strive for a balance of colors throughout the design; avoid isolated areas worked in a single color, especially one that is very bright.

In the lower right-hand corner of the finished sampler, write your name, and the date with a laundry marking pen and then embroider over the signature and date in Outline Stitch (4, page 542). When the sampler is completed, wash, press, or block, as necessary, and then mount it. (See Craftnotes, pages 546–547 and 548–549). For framing instructions, see "Framing" in Volume 6 .

Practicing the stitches: Before beginning the sampler, you may find it reassuring to practice the stitches (pages 542–545) on a scrap of linen. The stitches are numbered 1 to 36, each successive stitch building on the skills acquired in the preceding stitches. When practicing, start at stitch 1 and advance in sequence through stitch 36. Many of the illustrations for each stitch show the needle going in and out, in one step, for clarity.

Some stitches require a hand motion similar to that used in sewing and are done easily if the fabric is held loosely in the hand. Stitches that are worked best when the fabric is stretched tautly in a hoop are indicated by the symbol ▣ in the text accompanying the illustrations. For the correct way to embroider these stitches, see the Craftnotes at left, applicable to all forms of embroidery. These also show the proper way to thread the needle, and how to begin and end a yarn length.

Figure A: This is a full-size pattern for the crewelwork sampler pictured on page 539. ▶
Numbers key the 36 stitches; border blocks are keyed with names.

Simple Trellis

Pointed Leaf

Acorn

Tendril

Flower

Cross Stitched Trellis

Heart

Flowers

Two Leaves

Bell

Shells

Ovals

Waves

Cherries

Apple

Leaf

Diagonal Trellis

Trees

Rosebuds

Cat

Cactus

Cross Stitched Diagonal Trellis

A

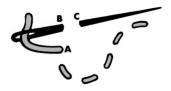

1. Running Stitch: Bring needle up at A, down at B, up at C. Space between stitches should be equal to their length.

2. Straight Stitch **:** Worked the same as running stitch, but the stitches are longer. May be worked in rows, at angles, or at random.

3. Backstitch: Work from right to left. Bring needle up at A; insert at B; bring it up at C, and draw thread through. Go back; insert in front of A, and complete figure. Be sure the stitch lengths are uniform.

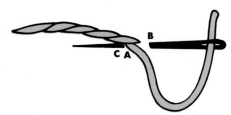

4. Outline or Stem Stitch: This is a basic stitch used to embroider lines, outlines and the stems of flowers. Start at top or bottom guide line. Bring needle up at A; insert at B at a slant as shown; bring up at C, and pull yarn through. Always keep the yarn on the same side of the needle.

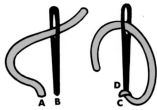

5. Seed Stitch : Small stitches randomly placed. Come up at A, go down at B, a small distance away. Come up at C and go down at D, crossing the first stitch diagonally.

6. Satin Stitch : A plump, solidly filled figure is created with this stitch. Outline the area to be worked with small Backstitches (3), to keep the edge even. Come up at A; draw yarn through. Go in at B; pull yarn through. Continue, placing stitches side by side across the design just outside the outline stitches. Keep the stitches close and their direction uniform.

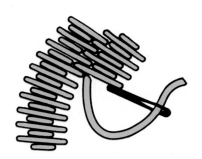

7. Long and Short Stitch : Resembles Satin Stitch (6) and is used to create a solid filling. Alternate long and short Satin Stitches, as shown, placing them side by side. In the next row, a long stitch goes below a short one.

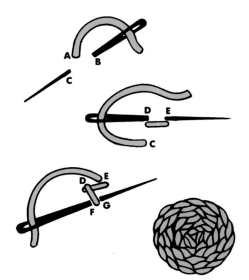

8. Raised Rose : Bring yarn up at A, and with needle at a slant, go in at B; come up at C; pull yarn through. Go in at D; come up at E; pull yarn through. Go in at F; come up at G; pull yarn through. Work a spiral of Outline Stitches (4) around triangle formed by first three steps.

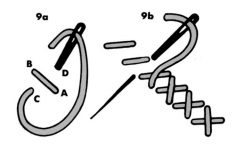

9a   **9b**

9. Cross Stitch: To make a single Cross Stitch, bring needle up at A; insert at B, up at C, and in at D, as in figure 9a. Be sure B and C, A and D are parallel. To make a row of Cross Stitches, work a row of slanting stitches from right to left, or left to right. Then work back across row, slanting stitches in the opposite direction, as in figure 9b. In a group of Cross Stitches, be sure the top stitches always slant in the same direction.

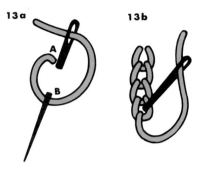

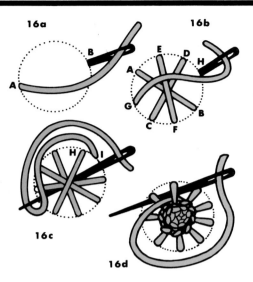

10. Herringbone Stitch: Row of slanted stitches crossed at top and bottom. Following the drawing, bring needle up at A, in at B, up at C, in at D, up at E, and continue.

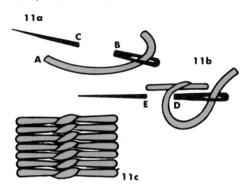

11. Roumanian Stitch: Bring needle up at A; pull yarn through. Go in at B and up at C, with thread below needle as in figure 11a. Pull yarn through. For second part of stitch, insert needle at D; bring out at E (figure 11b). Pull yarn through. Continue as from A. Result is shown in figure 11c.

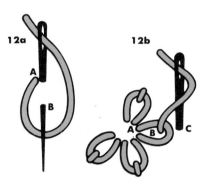

12. Lazy Daisy or Detached Chain: Bring the yarn up at A; make a loop and hold down loop with thumb. Insert the needle back at A and bring it out over the loop at B. Pull yarn through. Next, anchor the loop by inserting the needle at C and pulling the yarn through to the underside. May be worked separately as in figure 12a, but most often worked in a circle to form petals of a flower (figure 12b).

13. Chain Stitch: This stitch is also used for a decorative outline. Bring needle up at A; lay a loop of yarn on the fabric. Hold the loop while you insert the needle back at A and bring point of needle up at B, with loop held under point (figure 13a). Draw yarn through. Form remaining loops in same manner, always inserting needle where it emerged from last stitch (figure 13b). Anchor last stitch of chain by inserting the needle below its loop.

14. Open Chain: Made in the same way as the Chain Stitch (13) except the top of the loop is open. Finish off as for Chain Stitch.

15. Twisted Chain: Same as Open Chain (14), with a twist at the top of the loop.

16. Whipped Spider Web ◱: Work spokes with chenille or crewel needle. Bring needle up at A; insert at B, bisecting circle as in figure 16a. Bring needle up at C, pull yarn through and insert at D; up at E, in at F, up at G, and down at H, following figure 16b. Bring needle up at I (figure 16c). Change to tapestry needle. Slide tip of needle under all the threads where they cross at the center and loop the yarn over and under the needle tip as in figure 16c. Tighten yarn, forming a knot at the center, and the ninth spoke. To whip the spider (figure 16d), slide needle counterclockwise under two spokes of yarn (do not catch the fabric); pull yarn through; slide needle back under the second of these spokes and then under the spoke ahead, as shown. Pull yarn through. Continue in a spiral until the circle is filled.

17. Woven Spider Web ◱: This differs from Whipped Spider Web (16) in that the yarn is woven over and under single spokes counterclockwise. Work Whipped Spider to completion of center knot; then weave yarn under first spoke, over second, under third, continuing until circle is filled.

18. Backstitched Chain: Work a row of Chain Stitch; finish off. Using a contrasting color yarn, if desired, Backstitch (3) through it, as shown.

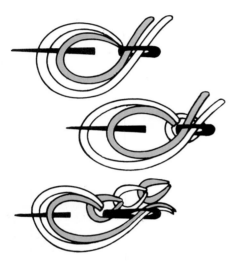

19. Magic Chain: Chain worked with two colors of yarn in the same needle. Thread needle with first and second colors, and proceed as for Chain Stitch (13), but loop only first color under the needle for the first stitch. For the second stitch, loop the second color under the needle. Alternate this pattern in subsequent stitches.

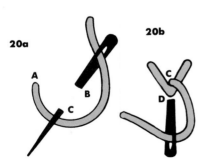

20. Fly Stitch: Like the Lazy Daisy Stitch (12), but open at top. Bring needle up at A; insert at B, and come up at C with the thread looped under the needle, as in figure 20a. Pull yarn through. Insert needle at D (figure 20b) to secure the loop.

21. Open Attached Fly Stitch: Like Fly Stitch (20), but anchored by a long rather than short stitch. Work from top to bottom.

22. Closed Attached Fly Stitch: Worked in the same manner as Open Attached Fly Stitch (21), but with the stitches close together and the connecting loops short.

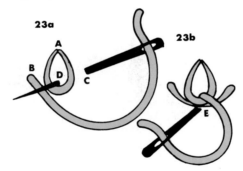

23. Wheat Ear Stitch: Combination of Lazy Daisy Stitch (12) and Fly Stitch (20). Bring needle up at A, form loop of desired size, and reinsert needle at A, as in Lazy Daisy Stitch (12). Bring the needle up at B and draw through. Insert needle at C and come up at D with yarn under needle (figure 23a). Pull through. Anchor at E (figure 23b).

24. Attached Wheat Ear: Complete Wheat Ear (23) through D, but do not anchor at E. Instead, make loop of next Wheat Ear, and then end by anchoring as in Wheat Ear.

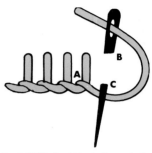

25. Blanket Stitch: Work from left to right. Bring needle up at A. Loop yarn in position shown, insert needle at B with point coming up at C and the yarn looped under needle. Draw yarn through. Repeat B-C across. This stitch can be used as a filling or to form outlines.

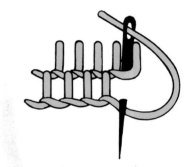

26. Attached Blanket Stitch: Joined rows of Blanket Stitch (25). Work row of Blanket Stitches. Finish off. Starting at the beginning of the row, work second row in bottom loops of first row. Work additional rows the same way.

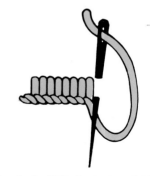

27. Buttonhole Stitch: A closed Blanket Stitch (25). Proceed as for Blanket Stitch, but space stitches close together, as shown.

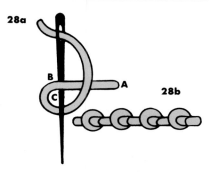

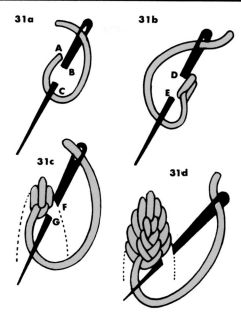

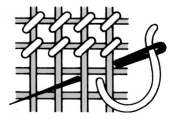

33. Simple Trellis ⬚: Trellises are squared filling stitches and consist of a combination of couching with preceding stitches. To couch means to tack down long threads with small stitches. Use long Straight Stitches (2) to lay evenly spaced trellises of yarn across area to be worked. Then couch intersections with small diagonal stitches as shown here.

28. Coral Stitch: Series of attached knots. Come up at point A. Hold yarn to the left; go in at point B, and come up at C with yarn under the needle. Draw knot tight. Lay thread to the left for next stitch. Continue as for B and C. Figure 28b shows a row of completed Coral Stitches.

29. French Knot: Come up at the point where the French Knot is to be. Form loop around needle, and insert needle vertically into or just next to same point. Pull loop tight around needle. Hold yarn with left thumb, pull needle through (figure 29a). Figure 29b shows enlarged finished French Knot.

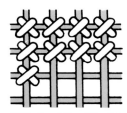

34. Cross Stitched Trellis ⬚: Worked as Simple Trellis (33), except the yarn is couched at intersections with small Cross Stitches (9).

31. Closed Cretan Stitch: Closely spaced, elongated loops that overlap. Work from top to bottom. Bring the needle up at A, in at B, and up at C with the yarn looped under the needle (figure 31a). Pull yarn through. Insert needle at D, and come up at E with yarn under the needle as in figure 31b. Pull yarn through. Next stitch, F to G (figure 31c), will begin just below and to the right of B. Pull yarn through, and continue. Increase the length of the stitches as you work downward (figure 31d).

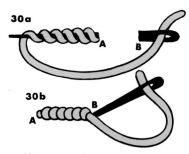

35. Simple Diagonal Trellis ⬚: Lay vertical and horizontal yarns as in Simple Trellis (33). Then lay diagonal yarns. Couch intersections with small diagonal stitches.

30. Bullion Stitch: Bring needle up at A. Insert needle at B and bring out near A; do not pull needle all the way through. Twist thread 6 times around point of needle as in figure 30a (the coils, when pushed together, should equal the distance between A and B). Holding coils and needle securely with thumb and forefinger, draw needle through fabric and coils. Carefully pull thread to tighten stitch so knot lies flat against the fabric (knot will flip over). Reinsert needle in B (figure 30b).

32. Open Cretan Stitch: Same as Closed Cretan Stitch (31), but with space between them.

36. Cross Stitched Diagonal Trellis ⬚: Lay yarns as in Simple Diagonal Trellis (35). Work diagonal rows of Outline Stitch (4), slanting in opposite direction from the first diagonals. Couch with Cross Stitches (9) where diagonals intersect.

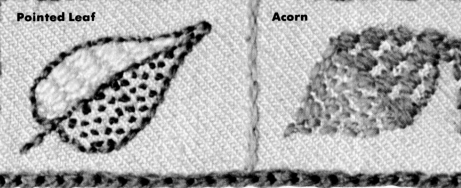

Simple Trellis

Pointed Leaf

Acorn

Heart

Flowers

Two Leaves

Upper left-hand corner of sampler.

The stitches used for the border of the top of the sampler are given on these two pages. To follow the instructions, start in the lower left corner of this page and work your way up and around the border in a clockwise direction. Methods of making the numbered stitches are given on pages 540 through 545.

Two Leaves: Both leaves are done in Cretan Stitch: the light green leaf is Closed Cretan Stitch (31); the dark green one is Open Cretan Stitch (32), and edged in Chain Stitch (13).

Flowers: French Knot (29) flowers are in four gradated shades of blue, light to dark. Stems are Outline Stitch (4) in blue.

Heart: Outer edge of heart is worked in Blanket Stitch (25) in light blue. Center is filled with rows of red Attached Blanket Stitch (26).

Simple Trellis: Each corner of the sampler is worked in a variation of this basic couched trellis, Simple Trellis (33). The trellis yarns are light green; the little couching stitches are light blue. The entire outside border of the sampler is worked in dark green Twisted Chain Stitch (15). The blocks are separated by Outline Stitch (4) in medium light blue. The inner border is worked in Chain Stitch (13) in medium blue.

Pointed Leaf: The shape of the leaf is delineated in medium blue Backstitch (3) as is the leaf's vein. Solid rows of light blue Backstitch fill the leaf's upper area. Lower half of the leaf is filled with dark green Seed Stitches (5).

EMBROIDERY CRAFTNOT

Washing and Pressing: If finished embroidery is soiled, wash with mild soap flakes in lukewarm water. Roll in a towel and let dry. Place face down on thick towel, cover with damp pressing cloth, and press with warm iron. If fabric still appears puckered, block as directed at right.

To Block Embroidery: Use a soft wood board larger than the piece to be blocked. Place a piece of aluminum foil the size of the background fabric on the board. This prevents the wood from staining the fabric, prevents water absorption, and serves as a pinning guide. Stretch the fabric taut over the foil.

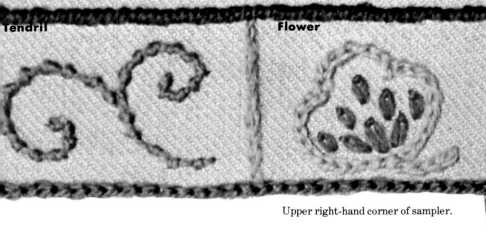

Tendril **Flower** **Cross Stitched Trellis**

Upper right-hand corner of sampler.

Acorn: Left side of acorn is worked in Running Stitch (1); right side and stem are in Straight Stitch (2). Yarn colors are two shades of gold.

Tendril: Curling tendril is worked entirely in Coral Stitch (28) in medium green yarn.

Flower: A delicate flower, outlined in Chain Stitch (15) worked in pink yarn, encircles a group of Lazy Daisy Stitches (14) worked in medium rose yarn.

Cross Stitched Trellis: This block is worked in Cross Stitched Trellis (34). The couched horizontal yarns are light green; the intersections are couched by Cross Stitches (9) with medium blue lower stitches and light blue upper stitches.

Ovals: Lines of inner and outer oval are embroidered in Magic Chain (19) with dark green and yellow yarns. Four dark green French Knots (29) fill the center.

Waves: The figure is worked in Twisted Chain (15) in light and dark greens.

Cherries: Leaf halves are worked in Satin Stitch (6) in two shades of gold. Cherry at right, also in Satin Stitch, is dark gold, one at left in Long and Short Stitch (7). The stems are Outline Stitch (4).

NISHING

Tack down the corners to the board with rustproof thumbtacks or push-pins. Tack down the centers of each side, halfway between the corners; keep stretching the fabric evenly. Continue placing tacks halfway between the previous tacks until they are about one-half inch apart. With warm water and a clean sponge, saturate the embroidery and background. Press paper toweling on it to remove excess. Allow to dry, away from heat and sunlight for 24 hours. Unpin.

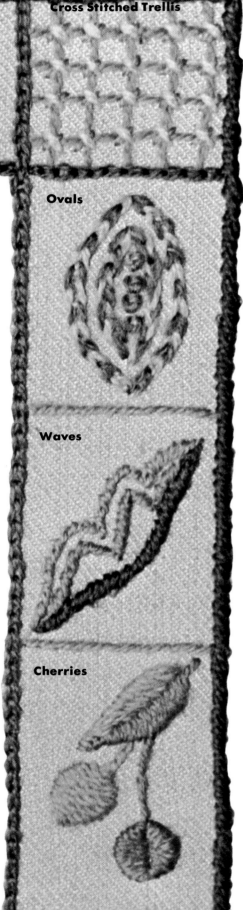

Ovals

Waves

Cherries

EMBROIDERY CRAFTNOTE

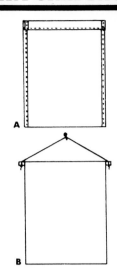

First Method

This is probably the simplest way to hang a piece of embroidery. For this method you will need a needle and thread or sewing machine, wooden doweling, and a length of yarn (optional). First, trim the background fabric if the edges are uneven. Make narrow hems at the sides by turning the edges under ¼ inch twice. Stitch a hem about 1 inch wide (the size depends upon the thickness of the dowel) at the top, leaving ends open (figure A). Cut a length of dowel about 2 inches longer than the width of the hanging, and insert in hem. Attach a length of yarn to the dowel at the top (figure B) or simply suspend embroidery from the dowel itself. If it is hanging smoothly, make a narrow hem at bottom. If you find that the hanging is curling or buckling, add weight to it by sewing another wide hem at the bottom and inserting another dowel.

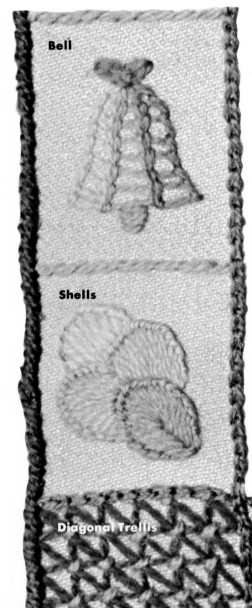

The stitches used for the border of the bottom of the sampler are given on these two pages. To follow the instructions, start at left and work your way down and around in a counter clockwise direction. Methods of making the numbered stitches are given on pages 540 through 545.

Bell: The bell is embroidered in Open Chain (16) in three shades of gold. The hanger is dark gold Chain Stitch (15); the clapper is Satin Stitch (6).

Shells: All four shell-like forms are worked in Buttonhole Stitch (27) in three shades of blue.

Diagonal Trellis: Another variation of a couched trellis, Diagonal Trellis (35). The horizontal and vertical yarns are dark green, the diagonals are dark rose. The couching stitches are gold.

Trees: Both figures are worked in Attached Fly Stitch; the light green tree is Closed Attached Fly Stitch (22); the dark green tree is worked in Open Attached Fly Stitch (21), with the stitches becoming progressively larger.

Rosebuds: Five rosebuds in shades of pink and rose. Clockwise starting from top left: pink, worked in Buttonhole Stitch (27); medium rose in Whipped Spider Web (12); medium rose in Woven Spider Web

Lower left-hand corner of sampler.

OUNTING

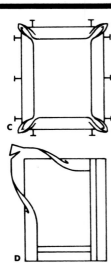

Second Method

To prepare embroidery for framing, stretch it on a board after blocking it. You will need heavy cardboard or ½-inch thick insulation board, straight pins, masking tape, and a staple gun (optional). Cut the board slightly smaller than the space at the back of the frame; allow ⅛ inch to ⅜ inch for heavy fabric. Place embroidery face down on a flat surface, and center the board on top. Fold fabric margins to the back, and insert straight pins into each side to secure fabric temporarily (figure C). Check to make sure that the threads of the fabric are even with the edges of the board. Tape top and bottom edges of the fabric to the board; trim fabric at corners if it seems too bulky; then tape down the sides (figure D). If the board is at least 3/16 inch thick, you can insert staples into the edges of the board, spacing them ¼ inch apart. This forms a more permanent mount, as the tape may dry up with time, allowing the fabric to sag.

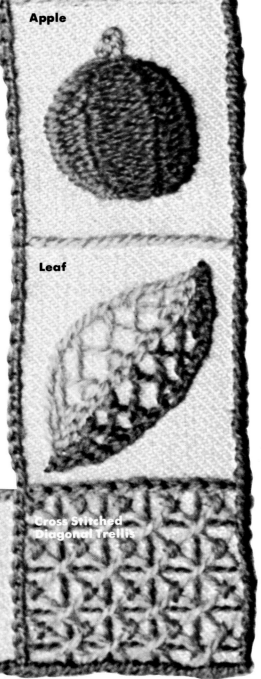

Apple

Leaf

Cross Stitched Diagonal Trellis

(13); dark rose in Woven Spider Web (13); medium rose in Raised Rose (8). Dark gold stem is Coral Stitch (30). Dark green snippet is Chain Stitch (15).

Cat: Three dark blue Wheat Ear Stitches (23) and a row of medium blue Attached Wheat Ears (24) flank a light blue cat in Coral Stitch (30) with Fly Stitch (20) ears and paws.

Cactus: Each spiky tip is a Bullion Stitch (32) in two shades of gold. The stems are Coral Stitch (30).

Cross Stitched Diagonal Trellis: The most complex of the corner trellises is Cross Stitched Diagonal Trellis (36). The horizontal and vertical yarns are dark green; the diagonals are light green with dark rose Cross Stitches (9) at the intersections.

Leaf: Each half of the leaf is worked in Herringbone Stitch (10); the left side is medium blue and the right side is dark green. The center line is a row of Backstitched chain (18) in medium blue and gold. Embroider the outline of the leaf in Chain Stitch (15) with dark green on the right side; in Outline Stitch (4) with medium blue on the left.

Apple: Roumanian Stitch (11), in three shades of rose, is worked in three rows to fill the apple. Stem, in aqua, is done in Chain Stitch (15).

For related projects, see "Applique," "Embroidery," and "Framing."

Lower right-hand corner of sampler.

Cat   Cactus

CROCHET
Magic With Stitchery

Brigitta Ansler was born and educated in Switzerland. In Schaffhausen, a town on the Rhine, and in Splugen, a small Alpine village, she was trained in home economics, including needle-work skills. With her husband, a Swiss architect, and four children, she now lives in Marblehead, Mass.

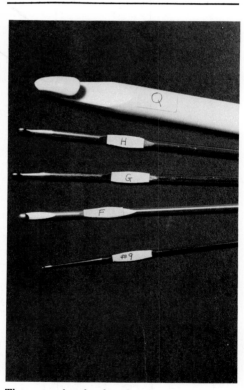

These crochet hooks, the sizes most often used, were needed for the projects on these pages. From the bottom: Five-inch steel hook, size 9, used with No. 20 crochet cotton for the pincushion. Three aluminum hooks, 5½ to 6 inches, suited to heavy wool yarns and acrylic; F used for the necktie, G for the bag, H for the dress. Eight-inch plastic hook, size Q, used to make the rug; also comes in wood.

Crochet is the French word for hook. Crocheted pieces are worked with a needle, like a knitting needle but hooked at one end. In the British Isles in the eighteenth century, crochet work was known as shepherd's knitting. In the sixteenth century, fine forms of crochet were used as trimming for church vestments and altar cloths. The earliest books of crochet patterns deal with these lacy forms, done with fine thread on fine hooks.

Hook size and the weight of the cotton or yarn used are related and determine the end product. For instance, the rug on the facing page and the tie on page 552 are worked in the same basic stitch, but sisal rope and a Q hook made the rug, while a size-F hook and four-ply worsted made the tie.

The crochet projects on these pages are planned so they will introduce the basic crochet stitches progressively. The stitches and the abbreviations used in crochet instructions are explained in the Craftnotes for "Afghan Stitch," pages 30 and 31, Volume One. By using only one of these stitches (except chain stitch) exclusively, an even-textured fabric results, as in the the tie, bag, and rug, pages 552, 553, and 557. Combinations of stitches produce open, lacy work, as on the dress sleeves, page 555. A variety of stitches produces intricate patterns, such as the pincushion, page 556.

Materials

Steel hooks sized 00 to 14 (with this type, higher numbers designate finer hooks) are used with cotton thread, ranging from sewing thread to stringlike weights, to crochet doilies, tablecloths, bedspreads, and the pincushion on page 556. Aluminum or plastic hooks are marked from D to K—or 1 to 10½, depending on the manufacturer (here, the higher the designation, the larger the hook). These are used for most of the projects described here and for sweaters, afghans, and hats. Wood hooks are sized 10 to 16. Giant wood or plastic hooks are designated Q to S.

Crochet hooks, thread, and yarn are sold in variety and department stores and knitting shops. The sisal rope used in the rug (opposite) is sold in large hardware stores. Sisal rope and the beads needed for the bag project on page 553 can be purchased by mail order from Naturalcraft, 2199 Bancroft Way, Berkeley, Cal. 94704.

Getting Started

To begin any crochet project, make a foundation of chain stitches. Following the diagramed stitches in the Craftnotes on page 30, Volume One, make a loop by hand, insert your crochet hook, and practice making a beginning chain stitch. Next, make a swatch of single-crochet stitch. Try to work with an even tension on the thread or yarn, so all similar stitches are the same size.

Before you start a crochet project, test your crocheting against the gauge given with the instructions. This gives the number of stitches and rows to an inch. Crochet a test piece 2 inches square. If it differs from the gauge, your result will not be the size specified. To check your test piece, count the horizontal stitches and vertical rows. If your sample has fewer stitches and rows to the inch than the gauge, make a new test swatch with the next smaller hook. If it has more stitches and rows, try the next larger hook.

To finish your work, cut the yarn 4 inches from the end. Draw the cut end through the last loop on the hook. Thread a yarn needle with this end, and weave the yarn for 2 inches on the wrong side of the work. Snip off excess yarn. Weave in all loose ends this way.

Finished pieces (except the rug) should be blocked—pinned to a padded surface and steamed with an iron at a Wool setting. Let dry before unpinning. For details of blocking, see Craftnotes for "Knitting To Fit," Volume Eight.

A warm, casual atmosphere is beautifully enhanced in this room by the color and texture of natural sisal rope. The crocheted-mesh rug, made by Brigitta Amsler, resists soil and is easily cared for by vacuuming. A square or rectangular rug of any size may be made with the directions on page 557.

Needlecrafts
Crocheted tie

When a craft is new to you, it is fun to make something that goes rapidly so the results can be enjoyed soon. This tie is a satisfying beginner's project because, worked with heavy worsted yarn and a size-F crochet hook, it is quickly finished. It could also be made with tweed yarn of the same weight.

Materials: 4 ounces 4-ply knitting worsted; 1 ounce mohair for trim. Crochet hook size F.

Gauge: 5 sc = 1 inch; 4 rows = 1 inch

Tie: Ch 6. *Row 1:* Sc in 2nd ch from hook and in each ch across. Ch 1, turn. *Row 2:* Sc in each sc across. Ch 1, turn (5 sc). Repeat this row until tie measures 31½". *Next row (inc row):* Work 2 sc in first sc, sc in each sc to last sc, 2 sc in last sc. Ch 1, turn. Repeat this row 6 times more. Work even on 19 sc until tie measures 20" from first inc row. Then dec 1 sc at each edge of every row until 1 sc remains. Fasten off.

Decoration: Attach mohair to wrong side of tie point. Following photograph for placement, work design as follows: Holding mohair on wrong side of work and crochet hook on right side, draw up a loop, * skip about ¼" of work, insert hook and draw up a loop and draw through loop on hook (a sl st), repeat from * keeping tension even. When design is completed, fasten off on wrong side. Press tie lightly.

Phyllis Neufelt has an art degree from Fresno State University, Cal. She teaches creative crochet at Community College in Merced, Cal., and designs abstract texture and fiber sculptures, wall hangings, and soft jewelry.

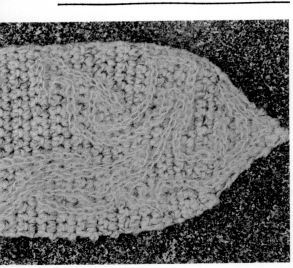

This close-up of the tie shows how the design was done at random with slip stitches in mohair yarn of a contrasting color, crocheted on after the body of the tie was finished.

Knitting worsted was used to crochet the necktie worn by this fanciful sandman. The tie is one flat piece made entirely of single-crochet stitches.

CROCHET

Needlecrafts
Beaded bag

This small clutch purse, decorated with brightly colored wooden beads, takes you a step further in learning to crochet. Here, you use three stitches: double crochet, slip stitch, and single crochet, pages 30 and 31, Volume One. The yarn is easy-to-work four-ply worsted. The hook used is G.

Materials: 2 ounces 4-ply knitting worsted; 95 wooden beads, Hook size G.

Gauge: 4 sc = 1 inch; 7 rows = 2 inches.

Body: Ch 22. **Row 1:** Sc in 2nd ch from hook and in each ch across. Ch 1, turn. **Row 2:** Sc in each sc across. Ch 1, turn. Repeat till 10″. Fasten off.

Flap: String 95 beads on yarn. Draw beads up as needed. Starting at center, ch 3. Join with sl st to first ch to form ring. **Rnd 1:** Work 8 sc in ring. Join with sl st. **Rnd 2:** * Sc in next sc, draw up a bead, sc in same sc; repeat from * around (16 sc, 8 beads). Join. **Rnd 3:** * Sc in next sc, draw up a bead; repeat from * around (16 sc, 16 beads). **Rnd 4:** Ch 3 to count as first dc, draw up a bead, dc at base of ch-3, * draw up a bead, dc in next sc, draw up a bead, dc in same sc; repeat from * around (32 dc, 32 beads). Ch 3 turn. **Rnd 5:** Dc in base of ch-3, dc in next 16 dc, 2 dc in next dc (20 dc). Ch 3, turn. **Rnd 6:** Work 2 dc in each dc with a bead next to each dc except last dc (40 dc, 39 beads). Fasten off.

Finishing: Sc flap to bag on right side. Fold bag body; sc sides.

CROCHET CRAFTNOTES

How to Crochet with Beads

Using yarn on which beads have been strung (see instructions at left), crochet the bead-bag flap up to the point where you begin to insert beads.

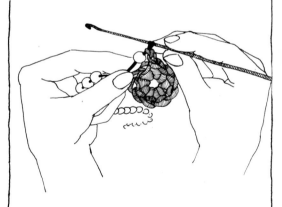

Draw a bead along the yarn, and place it beside the crochet hook. Then work a single-crochet stitch around the bead to secure it. Be sure to avoid any slack in the yarn that would let the bead hang loosely.

This beaded purse for a child is simple enough to be crocheted by the child. To make a handsome evening bag, use double strands of metallic yarn and simulated pearls.

553

Needlecrafts
Evening Dress

The evening dress pictured on the facing page is a good major project to undertake once your crocheting skills are secure. Although you are making a full-scale garment, this design avoids the complexities of fitting, a stumbling block for all but the most experienced crocheter. (Information on fitting handmade garments is given in "Knitting to Fit," Volume Eight.) Here, a lace-up-the-back closing (see figure A) contributes to making the dress fit most any figure from size 8 to size 16. This closing also precludes using a zipper, which would tend to make the soft garment buckle.

You start with the black worsted circle of the bodice. Then each section of the dress is crocheted directly onto finished parts, so there is no seaming to do. One side of the front and back is crocheted continuously onto the stitches on one side of the circle; the process is repeated on the other side. The skirt is crocheted from the bottom of the bodice downward. The shoulders are crocheted onto the bodice top last.

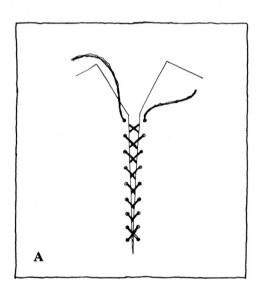

A

Figure A: This detail shows the lace-up-the-back closing. The tie, chain crocheted of one strand of each color of yarn, is laced through the sides of the back opening of the dress, just as shoes are laced.

Size: Fits sizes 8 to 16.

Materials: 24 ounces 4-ply knitting worsted in Color A; 8 grams imported sport-weight yarn with metallic thread in Color B. Crochet hook size H.

Gauge: 3 dc = 1 inch; 1 row = 1 inch.

Bodice Front: With Color A, ch 3. Join with sl st to form ring. **Rnd 1:** Ch 3, work 11 dc in ring. Join to ch-3. Ch 3, turn. **Rnd 2:** Dc at base of ch-3, work 2 dc in each dc around. Join—24 dc, counting ch-3 as 1 dc. Ch 3, turn. **Rnd 3:** Repeat Rnd 2— 48 dc. **Rnd 4:** Dc in each dc around. Join. Ch 3, turn. **Rnd 5:** * Work 2 dc in next dc, dc in next 5 dc; repeat from * around. Join—56 dc. Ch 3, turn. **Rnd 6:** * Dc in next 5 dc, 2 dc in next dc; repeat from * around. Join. Ch 3, turn. **Rnd 7:** * 2 dc in next 4 dc, dc in next dc; repeat from * around. Join. Ch 3, turn. **Rnd 8:** Sc in each dc around. Join. Ch 3, turn. **Rnd 9:** Dc in each sc around. Join. Fasten off. **Rnd 10:** With Color B, dc in each dc around. Join. Ch 3, turn. **Rnd 11:** Repeat Rnd 10. **Rnd 12:** Repeat Rnd 10. Fasten off. **Rnd 13:** With Color A, sc in each dc around. Join. Ch 2, turn.

Right Side of Bodice Back: Row 1: With Color A, sc in 17 sc. Ch 2, turn. Repeat row 24 times. Fasten off.

Left Side of Bodice Back: From bottom of right side, count 48 sts across waist of dress. **Row 1:** With A, sc in 17 sc. Ch 2, turn. **Row 2:** Sc in each sc across. Ch 2, turn.

Repeat 15 times. Fasten off.

Skirt: With Color A, starting in stitch where lower edge of left front attaches to bodice front, sc across front, right side, left side, join with sl st. Ch 2. turn. Repeat for a total of 10 rows. Fasten off. **Row 11:** With Color B, dc in each sc, sl st. Fasten off. **Row 12:** With Color A, dc in each dc, sl st. Ch 3, turn. **Rows 13 to 39:** Repeat Row 12 until desired length.

Edging: This consists of 5 rows of randomly spaced sets of dc sts. Ch sts are made between sets of dc. When same number of sts are skipped as chains are made, edging will be straight. If more chains are made between dcs, edging will be flouncy.

Left Shoulder: Skip 12 sts above left side. **Row 1:** With Color A, 1 dc in each of next 8 sts. Ch 3, turn. Repeat for 4 more rows, sl st to back. Fasten off.

Right Shoulder: Skip 12 sts above right side. **Row 1:** With Color A, 1 dc in each of next 8 sts. Ch 3, turn. Repeat for 4 more rows, sl st to back. Fasten off.

Sleeves: Row 1: With Color A, dc around armhole. Ch 3, turn. Edging consists of 15 rows of randomly spaced sets of dc sts. Ch sts are made between sets of dc. See edging instructions. Dec or inc the number of rows for desired length of sleeve

Tie: With Colors A and B held together, crochet a chain 4 yards long. Lace it up back of dress through holes in crochet, to close.

A close-up of the dress bodice shows the circle of black four-ply worsted that is the focal point of the bodice. This is where you start crocheting the dress. The other yarn used is a tweed with a metallic look.

The body of this complex-looking evening dress is crocheted with only single- and double-crochet stitches. The lacy edging on the sleeves and a matching one on the skirt is made with the same stitches, plus chain stitch. The dress can be made as long as desired simply by working additional rows on the skirt before crocheting the edging.

Needlecrafts
Irish-crochet pincushion

Marguerite Dickson has been crocheting for more than 60 years. She particularly enjoys doing lacy work on doilies, scarves, and edgings. Mrs. Dickson lives in San Francisco.

The crochet stitches used in the preceding projects, combined with treble crochet (page 31, Volume One), are used to make this Irish-crochet pincushion, which is approximately 10 inches across. It requires care, since it is a little tricky to keep track of where you are in the pattern. If you lose your place and make a mistake, you can correct it only by ripping it out and reworking that section.

Irish crochet is an adaptation of Venetian rose-point lace developed by Irishwomen during the potato famine of the 1840s as a means of earning money. The rose motif of the pincushion on this page is one of the traditional favorites. It is made with a size-9 hook and ecru crochet cotton No. 20.

To make the pincushion, crochet the cover, following instructions below; then ready the pincushion. You will need: a handful of polyester filler; a 12-inch square of fuchsia felt; ½ yard of 1-inch-wide fuchsia grosgrain ribbon; a 7½-by-2-inch circle of foamed plastic; white glue; straight pins; scissors.

Mound the surface of the foam circle with 1-inch-deep polyester filler. Drape the felt over the padded foam; then pin in place. Cut away excess felt. Pin the ribbon around the bottom edge with half the ribbon's width up the side and the other half underneath. A few inches at a time, unpin the ribbon; apply glue to the wrong side; pin ribbon back in place. Let the glue dry; remove pins. Position finished crochet cover over the padded, felt-covered foamed plastic and sew in place with tiny running stitches.

Size: Approximately 10 inches.
Materials: 1 (300-yard) ball mercerized crochet cotton No. 20. Steel crochet hook size 9.

Irish Crochet Pincushion Cover: Starting at center, ch 6. Join with sl st to form the ring. **Rnd 1:** Ch 6, dc in ring, * ch 3, dc in ring; repeat from * 3 times more, ch 3, join with sl st to 3rd ch of ch-6. **Rnd 2:** Ch 1, * work 2 dc, 5 tr and 2 dc in next sp, sc in next dc; repeat from * around. Join (6 petals made). **Rnd 3:** * Ch 6, sc in next sc in back of petal; repeat from * around. Join. **Rnd 4:** Ch 1, * work 2 dc, 7 tr, 2 dc over next ch-6, sc in next sc; repeat from * around. Join (6 petals made). **Rnd 5:** Ch 10, sl st in 5th ch from hook for picot, ch 7, sl st in 5th ch from hook for picot, ch 2, sc in center st of next petal, * (ch 7, sl st in 5th ch from hook for picot) twice, ch 2, dc in sc between petals, (ch 7, sl st in 5th ch from hook for picot) twice, ch 2, sc in center of next petal; repeat from * 4 times (ch 7, sl st in 5th ch from hook for picot) twice, ch 2. Join to 3rd ch of starting chain. **Rnd 6:** * Ch 7, sc between picots of next loop, ch 7, sc in next sc, ch 7, sc between picots of next loop, ch 7, sc in next dc; repeat from * around. Join. **Rnd 7:** Sl st to center of next loop, * ch 7, sc in next loop; repeat from * around. Join. **Rnd 8:** Repeat Rnd 7. **Rnd 9:** Work 1 sc, 7 dc and 1 sc in next loop (shell made), ch 1, work 1 sc, 7 dc and 1 sc in next loop, * (ch 7, sl st in 5th ch from hook for picot) twice, ch 2, sc in next loop; repeat from * once, (ch 7, sl st in 5th ch from hook for picot) twice, ch 2 (double picot loop made); repeat from * around. Join. **Rnd 10:** Sl st to center of shell, * ch 7, sc in center of next shell, (ch 7, sc between 2 picots of next loop) 3 times, ch 7, sc in center of next shell; repeat from * around. Join. **Rnd 11:** * Work 1 sc, 7 dc and 1 sc in next loop, (make double picot loop, sc in next loop) 4 times, make double picot loop; repeat from * around. Join. **Rnd 12:** Sl st to center of next shell, * (ch 7, sc between picots of next loop) 5 times, ch 7, sc in center of next shell; repeat from * around. Join. **Rnd 13:** * Work 1 sc, 7 dc and 1 sc in next loop, (make double picot loop, sc in next loop) 5 times, work 7 dc and 1 sc in same loop, ch 1; repeat from * around. Join. **Rnd 14:** Sl st to center of next shell, (ch 7, sc between picots of next loop) 5 times, ch 7, sc in center of next shell. Continue in this manner around. For a lacy edge, make 3 double picot sts in one loop (ch 7, sl st in 2nd ch from hook). Then make 2 chains of 5 ch sts in single loop and 3 chains of 5 ch sts in every third loop. Fasten off.

Needlecrafts
Crocheted sisal rug

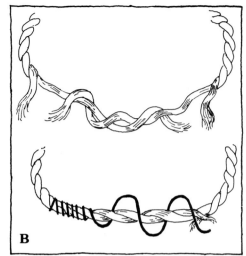

B

With the simplest crochet stitches, a wonderfully textured room-size or area rug can be made with natural sisal rope (photograph, page 551). The rug is especially suited to a beach house, recreation room, porch, or patio as it resists soil and its open construction lets sand sift through. You will need two-ply sisal rope (³/₁₆ inch in diameter), available at craft and hardware stores in spools or reels weighing up to 50 pounds. For the 10-by-10-foot rug pictured, I used two and a quarter 50-pound spools and spliced ends twice.

A guide in purchasing rope is to allow one to one and a quarter pounds of rope for each square foot of rug. How much you will actually use depends on how tightly you crochet. Crochet a foot-square sample, and weigh it to check the amount of rope you used. When you need to splice rope from a new spool, untwist a few inches of each rope end; trim one ply (strand) of each a few inches, and twist the two longer plies together. Bind the twist with buttonhole cord for a smooth joint (figure B).

The wood crochet hook used to make the rug shown is Swiss. It is sketched in figure C, together with two American wood hooks available at most needlework shops. American hooks can be modified to work efficiently with the sisal material. Sandpaper them to a smooth, narrow shape resembling the Swiss hook. A deepened groove, narrow head, and very smooth surface help the stitches go quickly. A plastic hook, size Q, can also be used (photograph, page 550). It is smooth and has a fairly open groove. The hook and cotton gloves to protect your hands from rope abrasion are all the equipment you need for this project. To avoid turning over the entire rug for each row, spread the work over a table, and move from one side of the table to the other.

Decide on the size of the finished rug. It can be square or rectangular. To begin, make a row of chain stitches measuring about 2 inches more than the rug's short side, or width. This allows for bulk in the following rows.

First row: Ch 1 to turn, and sc into one side of each st in the ch. ***Pattern row:*** Ch 1 to turn, and sc into one side of each sc in preceding row. Repeat pattern until the rug is the desired size. ***Last row:*** Sl st into one side of each sc in preceding row. ***Edging:*** Ch 1 to turn corner, and sc into each turning ch along rug length. Across starting end, sl st into each ch. Ch 1 to turn corner, and sc into each turning ch along opposite length.

For related projects, see the entries "Afghan Stitch," "Granny Squares," and "Knitting To Fit."

Figure B;   Two sketches show details of joining sisal-rope ends by splicing. At the top, rope ends from the two spools have been unraveled; one strand from each has been cut short, and the long strands are being twisted together. At the bottom, joined strands are being bound with sturdy buttonhole cord, which will be knotted into place.

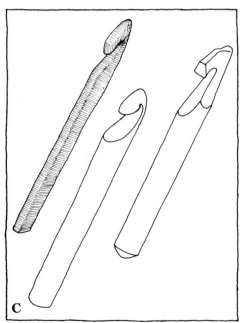

C

Figure C: The wood Swiss crochet hook, left, is the best one with which to make the sisal rug. It can be reproduced by sanding the sharp edges of either of the two American hooks, size Q, at right.

This is a detail of Brigitta Amsler's rug, pictured on page 551. Three of the simplest crochet stitches make it: the foundation is chain stitch; single crochet forms the body, slip stitch finishes the ends. No blocking or shaping is required.

CRYPTOGRAPHY
Find the Hidden Message

Consultant for this article is Barbara Harris, a computer programmer whose interest in codes and ciphers began when she joined a cryptography club at the age of twelve. A member of the American Cryptogram Association, she has worked as a consultant on several books that have required codebreaking expertise.

A	⊙	Sun	O	♍ Virgo
B	♃	Jupiter	P	♎ Balance (Libra)
C	♄	Saturn	Q	♏ Scorpion
D	♆	Neptune	R	♐ Sagittarius
E	♅	Uranus	S	♑ Capricorn
F	⊕	Earth	T	♓ Fishes
G	♀	Venus	U	♈ Ram
H	♂	Mars	V	♒ Aquarius
I	☿	Mercury	W	>
J	☾	Moon	X	≫
K	♉	Taurus	Y	⊢
L	♊	Twins	Z	<
M	♋	Cancer		
N	♌	Lion		**A**

Figure A: In the Zodiac Alphabet, the ciphers in the center column represent both letters and the names of planets or constellations.

OBONCE OBUPOBON OBA TOBIME THOBERE WOBERE THROBEE BOBEARS . . . Can you read this partial message? In its uncoded form, it could be read easily by any five-year-old. The words have been deliberately altered in a very simple way for the purposes of secrecy. The message, "Once upon a time, there were three bears," is obvious, once you know the method. In this secret language of OB, the letter-pair *OB* is inserted before every pronounced vowel, including *Y*. The words that would follow, translated into OB, would read like this: MOBAMOBA BOBEAR POBAPOBA BOBEAR OBAND BOBABOBY BOBEAR. Absurd as it looks (and sounds, as it can be spoken as well as written), it represents a very crude form of secret writing, or *cryptography* (from the Greek, *kryptos*, secret, and *graphos*, writing). If you figured it out without knowing the key beforehand, you were practicing *cryptanalysis*.

Not all codes are designed to convey secret messages, of course. While they may be cryptic to the uninitiated, the Morse and Semaphore codes (pages 564–565) are basically systems for speeding messages over distances rather than hiding them. But the purpose (and fun) of cryptography is to keep the message hidden by using codes and ciphers known only to the sender and intended receiver. The word *code* is commonly used in a generic sense to refer to both codes and ciphers, and you will often find the words *code* and *cipher* are used interchangeably. But cryptographers make a precise distinction between the two. The first means working with entire words; the second with the letters of those words.

The Cryptographer's Vocabulary and Methods

In the language of modern cryptography, the message to be sent is called the *plaintext*. After the plaintext has been transformed by cryptography, it is referred to as the *codetext* or *ciphertext*. Putting a plaintext into codetext is called *encoding*; while putting a plaintext into cipher form is called *enciphering*. To break a code is to *decode* and to break a cipher system is to *decipher*.

Cryptographers transform plaintext into codes and ciphers in two basic ways. The first is *transposition* in which the words or letters of the plaintext are written in an order different from their actual one. In the OB language, the letters are made to seem transposed by the insertion of other letters. In another example, the word NORMAL may become ALRMNO when the letters are shuffled in a pattern. You may have seen such exercises in your daily newspaper as word jumbles. Both methods are too simple for serious cryptographers.

The second method is *substitution* in which the words or letters of the plaintext correspond to other words, letters, symbols, or numbers. In a code, a set of letters, a word, or a group of words is taken as a basic unit and is assigned a meaning known only to the persons transmitting and receiving the messages. If the codetext were *the three bears*, the entire phrase might represent a plaintext phrase such as "Intercept enemy courier." Or, as we will see below when we come to creating a codebook vocabulary, *bears* could be assigned an arbitrary numerical equivalent such as *1234*. Since such codes are not very secure, most modern cryptographers use ciphers instead.

Codes and Ciphers

In a cipher system, a single letter is used as the basic unit to be transformed. Each letter of a plaintext phrase, such as *the three bears*, would be replaced by a letter, symbol, or number in the ciphertext. As a simple example, using alphabetical equivalents to the numbers 1–26, *the* could be enciphered as *20,8,5*. Medieval philosophers, alchemists and astrologers used the Zodiac Alphabet, shown at left, as a substitution cipher which they hoped would keep others from learning their secret knowledge.

A message that has undergone substitution might then undergo transposition as well. When these two methods are combined, the process is called *superencipherment*. Although this makes a message more difficult to break, and thus more secure, it also requires more time to decipher.

Thousands of secret messages have strewn the paths of history since the invention of language. Rulers and politicians have always found codes and ciphers to be basic tools of diplomacy and intrigue. Sometimes their secret messages betrayed them, as was the case with Mary, Queen of Scots, pictured at right, who was beheaded for treason in 1587. Good cryptographers realize that secret writing is only as secure as it is secret. For this reason, they try to make their systems so complicated that they won't be broken for long periods of time. For further security, they regularly change the system, or the key to it, so codebreakers will be thwarted again and again.

Toys and Games
Making and breaking codes

To work well, a code must have thousands of plaintext words or phrases with a codetext equivalent for each. Usually, for the sake of manageability, a codetext word is limited to three to five letters or numbers. All the codetexts and their plaintext meanings are listed in a codebook.

Cryptographers work with one-part and two-part codes. A one-part code requires only one codebook for encoding and decoding. All the plaintexts are listed alphabetically beside their codetext equivalents, which are also listed in alphabetical or numerical order. To make a one-part codebook, like the partial sample below, first go through a dictionary and list the words you want to use, then assign a codetext meaning to each word. Next, list all the plaintexts in order in the codebook with their codetexts beside them. Since you will use the book for both encoding and decoding, make one codebook for each person using the code.

Heir apparent to the English throne, Mary, Queen of Scots (shown here with son, James) was kept under house arrest by Queen Elizabeth I for many years. During this time Mary engaged in secret plots to have Elizabeth assassinated. Foolishly, she tried cryptographic correspondence, thinking that her messages would go undiscovered. But Mary made two mistakes: she used a simple substitution cipher system that was easily broken and she trusted a courier who was a double agent. When Mary's conspiracy could no longer be tolerated, the deciphered incriminating messages were shown to Elizabeth and Mary was tried, found guilty, and beheaded.

One-Part Codebook

Plaintext	Codetext
A	0001
ABANDON	0002
ABLE	0003
ACCIDENT	0004
ADDRESS	0005
AFFORD	0006
AIR	0007
ALARM	0008

B

Two-Part Codebook

Encoding Book		Decoding Book	
Plaintext	Codetext	Codetext	Plaintext
ARRIVING	1849	0217	FINAL
BOMB	0617	0617	BOMB
COURIER	2601	1174	WITH
DESTROY	1246	1246	DESTROY
ENEMY	2999	1849	ARRIVING
FINAL	0217	2601	COURIER
STOP	2889	2889	STOP
WITH	1174	2999	ENEMY

C

Figure B: A one-part codebook: plaintext is listed alphabetically; codetext numerically.

Figure C: In the encoding book, left, plaintexts appear alphabetically. In the decoding book, right, plaintexts are jumbled and codetexts appear in numerical sequence.

A two-part code requires two codebooks, one for encoding and one for decoding as shown above, right. In the encoding book, the plaintexts are listed alphabetically beside their codetext equivalents, but the codetexts have no order at all. In the decoding book, the codetexts are listed in numerical (or alphabetical) order, but the plaintexts are necessarily scrambled. If you make a two-part code, you must make two codebooks for each person using the code. Using the sample two-part codebook above, decode this message: 0617 1849 1174 2601.

Making a good code is quite a job as you can see. As we proceed, you will also understand why codes are not the most secure form of secret writing. If you lose your codebook, you can no longer use the code. If a codebook falls into the wrong hands, an entirely new code, with new codebooks, must be made.

Code 0075

In 1917, the United States' entry into World War I was hastened by the solving of a single coded telegram, shown below. On January 16, 1917, Alfred Zimmerman, the German Foreign Secretary, sent the coded message via his embassy in Washington, to the German Minister in Mexico. The British intercepted the note, broke the code, and eventually delivered the message to United States officials. The Americans were stunned; Germany was proposing that Mexico enter the war against the United States. Mexico's reward was to be New Mexico, Texas and Arizona. Faced with this threat, the United States promptly declared war on Germany.

The British cryptanalysts spent more than six months breaking the code of the

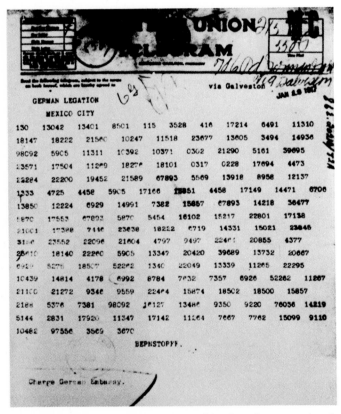

The Zimmerman Note was a unique example of a combination of a one-part and a two-part code. Intercepted and decoded by the British in 1917, it was a factor in the U.S. entry into World War I.

Zimmerman Note. It was Code 0075, a numerical code with about 10,000 words and phrases.

To solve a code of any kind, the cryptanalyst must discover the plaintexts for the vital codetexts. A one-part code offers a major clue because the plaintexts and the codetexts are in the same kind of order. Low-number codetexts correspond to plaintexts near the beginning of the alphabet, and high toward the end of the alphabet.

To break a two-part code, the analyst must depend on other clues. If he knows the subject matter covered, he has a clue. He must then try to discover codetexts that appear often. Above all, he must have a great many coded messages to work with.

The British had many messages in Code 0075, but the code was unusual, a cross between a one- and a two-part code. In the encoding book, all the plaintexts were listed alphabetically, but their codetexts were listed in numerical blocks. While the numbers were in order within each block, the blocks were jumbled. For example, words between *able* and *barrage* might go from 6514 to 6953, while those from *brave* to *city* could be from 3922 to 4237.

Survival Skills
Devising and solving ciphers

In a cipher system, each letter of the plaintext can be replaced by any other letter or number. A substitution cipher requires an alphabet in which all the letters are rearranged. Their order can be completely random, but it is usually determined by a key word.

Substitution Ciphers

Method I: The word DICTIONARY will be the key word. Write the key word, leaving out any letters that repeat, in this case, the second I. Then write the remaining letters of the alphabet after the key word. Leave out the letters of the alphabet already used in the key word, which are, D, I, C, T, O, N, A, R, Y; then proceed to list the remainder of the alphabet in the usual order:

Key word:	**DICTIONARY**
Cipher alphabet:	**D I C T O N A R Y B E F G H J K L M P Q S U V W X Z**
Plaintext alphabet:	**A B C D E F G H I J K L M N O P Q R S T U V W X Y Z**

This brass cipher disk was used by cryptographers of the Confederate Army during the Civil War. The inner circle could be rotated, serving as a codebook, when messages were encoded and decoded.

Problem 1

Using the plaintext alphabet above, what would be the cipher for the message, RUSH REPLY? (All answers to problems are given on page 565.)

Method II: Use the word DICTIONARY again, and dropping the second I, write out the word. Write the rest of the alphabet in rows beneath it. To produce the cipher alphabet, read down each column, working from left to right, and write the resulting sequence of letters, as shown.

Key Word:	**DICTIONARY**
	D I C T O N A R Y
	B E F G H J K L M
	P Q S U V W X Z
Cipher alphabet:	**D B̲ P I E̲ Q C F S T G U O H V N J W A K X R L Z Y̲ M**
Plaintext alphabet:	**A B̲ C D E̲ F G H I J K L M N O P Q R S T U V W X Y̲ Z**

Problem 2

Using this cipher alphabet, what is the plaintext for LDSK XHKSU IDWG? If any letter repeats itself in the cipher alphabet, such as B, E, and Y (underscored above), cryptographers sometimes shift the plaintext alphabet to the left or right to make the cipher more difficult to break. Both methods are easy to use. When you encipher or decipher a message, simply remember the key word and write out the alphabet. Frequent changing of the key word preserves security.

Problem 3

Using Method 1 and the key word, CRYPTOGRAPHY, make a cipher alphabet. Encipher this message: *Send agent to headquarters.*

Problem 4

Decipher this message, again using CRYPTOGRAPHY as the key word: CEEKT MNJII TEASI QHIGE TCPTM JONKX MHIG

Polyalphabetic Ciphers

A cipher is called polyalphabetic when more than one alphabet is used to encipher and decipher. The most famous example of a polyalphabetic cipher is the Purple Cipher, used during World War II by the Japanese in the decoded message pictured at right.

From: Tokyo
To: Washington
7 December 1941
(Purple-Eng)

#902   Part 14 of 14

(Note: In the forwarding instructions to the radio station handling this part, appeared the plain English phrase "VERY IMPORTANT")

7. Obviously it is the intention of the American Government to conspire with Great Britain and other countries to obstruct Japan's efforts toward the establishment of peace through the creation of a New Order in East Asia, and especially to preserve Anglo-American rights and interests by keeping Japan and China at war. This intention has been revealed clearly during the course of the present negotiations. Thus, the earnest hope of the Japanese Government to adjust Japanese-American relations and to preserve and promote the peace of the Pacific through cooperation with the American Government has finally been lost.

The Japanese Government regrets to have to notify hereby the American Government that in view of the attitude of the American Government it cannot but consider that it is impossible to reach an agreement through further negotiations.

JD-1:7143   SECRET   (M) Navy trans. 7 Dec. 1941 (S-TT)
25843

60   42

UNCLASSIFIED Published in Joint Committee Print, 79th Cong. 1st Session, Pearl Harbor Jt. Committee on the Investigation of Pearl Harbor Attack. U.S. Government Printing Office, Washington- 1945

Shown in its deciphered form, the last part of a 14-part message from Japan to its Washington embassy told of a break in relations with the United States. It was originally written in the Purple Cipher, a system of alphabet tables keyed by a cipher machine that took American cryptanalysts 20 months to decipher.

Vigenere Cipher

The Vigenere Cipher is one of the oldest polyalphabetic ciphers. It's 26 alphabets are all written in the usual sequence. A short, repeating key word is used. The Vigenere table illustrated below is composed as follows: Write the plaintext alphabet across the top of your page; then write it vertically down the left side, as the key alphabet. Under the first horizontal row, write the alphabet in normal order. This is the A-alphabet. In the next row, write the alphabet beginning with B. Place the A after the Z. Begin each row with the succeeding letter, and, at the end, add the letters omitted at the beginning. You will have 26 rows: A-alphabet through Z-alphabet.

The key word must be chosen. Each of its letters represents one of the key alphabets in the table. The key word, SHOW, for example, uses 4: the S, H, O, and W-alphabets. To encipher the plaintext word, *neat*, using SHOW as the key word, first write the key word SHOW. Below it, write the plaintext, *neat*. Each letter of the plaintext must be enciphered with the alphabet for the key letter above it. Thus, *n* will be enciphered with the S-alphabet, *e* with the H, *a* with the O, and *t* with the W.

Put the point of a pencil on the *n* in the plaintext alphabet at the top of the table. Move the pencil down the vertical column beneath the *n* until you reach the row that begins (at the far left) with an S. The letter at the juncture is F. This is the cipher for *n*. To find the cipher for the *e* of neat, run your pencil down the column headed with plaintext *e* until you reach the row that begins with H. The cipher is L. When you have enciphered the *a* and the *t*, you should have the word *flop*. To decipher, reverse the procedure. Find the key letter to the ciphertext letter in the key alphabet at left. Follow across the row to the ciphertext letter; follow up that column to the plaintext letter heading that column. By simply changing the key

Figure D: The Vigenere alphabetic table looks like a simple system at first glance, but it is often referred to as *le chiffre indechiffrable* ("the undecipherable cipher") because it is so difficult to break. It is named for the Frenchman Blaise de Vigenere who, though he did not invent it, was credited with first describing the system. ▶

Plaintext Alphabet

	A	B	C	D	E	F	G	H	I	J	K	L	M	N	O	P	Q	R	S	T	U	V	W	X	Y	Z
A	A	B	C	D	E	F	G	H	I	J	K	L	M	N	O	P	Q	R	S	T	U	V	W	X	Y	Z
B	B	C	D	E	F	G	H	I	J	K	L	M	N	O	P	Q	R	S	T	U	V	W	X	Y	Z	A
C	C	D	E	F	G	H	I	J	K	L	M	N	O	P	Q	R	S	T	U	V	W	X	Y	Z	A	B
D	D	E	F	G	H	I	J	K	L	M	N	O	P	Q	R	S	T	U	V	W	X	Y	Z	A	B	C
E	E	F	G	H	I	J	K	L	M	N	O	P	Q	R	S	T	U	V	W	X	Y	Z	A	B	C	D
F	F	G	H	I	J	K	L	M	N	O	P	Q	R	S	T	U	V	W	X	Y	Z	A	B	C	D	E
G	G	H	I	J	K	L	M	N	O	P	Q	R	S	T	U	V	W	X	Y	Z	A	B	C	D	E	F
H	H	I	J	K	L	M	N	O	P	Q	R	S	T	U	V	W	X	Y	Z	A	B	C	D	E	F	G
I	I	J	K	L	M	N	O	P	Q	R	S	T	U	V	W	X	Y	Z	A	B	C	D	E	F	G	H
J	J	K	L	M	N	O	P	Q	R	S	T	U	V	W	X	Y	Z	A	B	C	D	E	F	G	H	I
K	K	L	M	N	O	P	Q	R	S	T	U	V	W	X	Y	Z	A	B	C	D	E	F	G	H	I	J
L	L	M	N	O	P	Q	R	S	T	U	V	W	X	Y	Z	A	B	C	D	E	F	G	H	I	J	K
M	M	N	O	P	Q	R	S	T	U	V	W	X	Y	Z	A	B	C	D	E	F	G	H	I	J	K	L
N	N	O	P	Q	R	S	T	U	V	W	X	Y	Z	A	B	C	D	E	F	G	H	I	J	K	L	M
O	O	P	Q	R	S	T	U	V	W	X	Y	Z	A	B	C	D	E	F	G	H	I	J	K	L	M	N
P	P	Q	R	S	T	U	V	W	X	Y	Z	A	B	C	D	E	F	G	H	I	J	K	L	M	N	O
Q	Q	R	S	T	U	V	W	X	Y	Z	A	B	C	D	E	F	G	H	I	J	K	L	M	N	O	P
R	R	S	T	U	V	W	X	Y	Z	A	B	C	D	E	F	G	H	I	J	K	L	M	N	O	P	Q
S	S	T	U	V	W	X	Y	Z	A	B	C	D	E	F	G	H	I	J	K	L	M	N	O	P	Q	R
T	T	U	V	W	X	Y	Z	A	B	C	D	E	F	G	H	I	J	K	L	M	N	O	P	Q	R	S
U	U	V	W	X	Y	Z	A	B	C	D	E	F	G	H	I	J	K	L	M	N	O	P	Q	R	S	T
V	V	W	X	Y	Z	A	B	C	D	E	F	G	H	I	J	K	L	M	N	O	P	Q	R	S	T	U
W	W	X	Y	Z	A	B	C	D	E	F	G	H	I	J	K	L	M	N	O	P	Q	R	S	T	U	V
X	X	Y	Z	A	B	C	D	E	F	G	H	I	J	K	L	M	N	O	P	Q	R	S	T	U	V	W
Y	Y	Z	A	B	C	D	E	F	G	H	I	J	K	L	M	N	O	P	Q	R	S	T	U	V	W	X
Z	Z	A	B	C	D	E	F	G	H	I	J	K	L	M	N	O	P	Q	R	S	T	U	V	W	X	Y

Key Word Alphabet

D

word, different alphabets can be used to encipher. With the key word FIVE, the cipher message is different:

If the key word is:	**F I V E**
and the plaintext word is:	**N E A T**
then the ciphertext is:	**S M V X**

You have now learned the basics of polyalphabetic ciphers. Usually the letters of a message are transmitted in groups of five letters, with no distinctions made between the beginnings and ends of words. For example, the sentence "Secret agent Bond will arrive incognito" must be divided into five-letter groups before it is enciphered and will than read: "Secre tagen tBond willa rrive incog nito." We will encipher this message, using CENTER as the key word. Write the letters of the key word in groups of five, corresponding to the letter groupings of the plaintext message.

Key word:	**CENTER**					
	CENTE	RCENT	ERCEN	TERCE	NTERC	ENTER CENTE
Plaintext:	SECRE	TAGEN	TBOND	WILLA	RRIVE	INCOG NITO
Ciphertext:	UIPKI	KCKRG	XSQRQ	PMCNE	EKMMG	MAVSX PMGH

Now decipher the message below, using the same key word (CENTER). Remember that in deciphering you are working from ciphertext to plaintext. Find the ciphertext letter in the Vigenere table opposite, indicated by the key letter, and follow up the row to the plaintext alphabet to decipher each letter.

Key word:	**CENTER**					
	CENTE	RCENT	ERCEN	TERCE	NTERC	ENTER C
Ciphertext:	DSAWM	JJIEX	EJRIE	IPRPW	FXRKV	YRLHR A
Plaintext:	BONDI	SHERE	ASPER	PLANS	SENTT	UESDA Y

As you can see, the alphabets repeat when the key word has repeated letters. This makes the message more vulnerable to analysis and should be avoided.

The Playfair Cipher

In the cipher systems mentioned so far, the plaintext has been enciphered one letter at a time. With the Playfair Cipher, however, single letters are replaced by pairs of letters in the ciphertext. Used by the British as a field cipher in World War I, the Playfair Cipher is monoalphabetic. The cipher alphabet is set in a five-by-five letter square with the J dropped. The J is replaced by an I in the plaintext whenever it is needed.

To make the cipher alphabet, write a key word, such as CALIFORNIA, omitting repeated letters. Then write the rest of the alphabet after the key, leaving out J and the letters already in the key. (See Figures E, F, G, at right.)

To use the Playfair Cipher, write the plaintext message in pairs of letters. If any letters repeat, replace them with an X, or insert an X between them. Add an X at the end if you have an uneven number of letters. Each pair of letters is then substituted by one of the three methods described at the right.

The message "Come later" is enciphered as follows:

Plaintext:	CO	ME	LA	TE	RX
Ciphertext:	OE	EG	IL	EK	NW

Using the same key, the following is deciphered:

Ciphertext:	QC	IE	RQ	HP	HO	SY
Plaintext:	PA	CK	AG	ES	EN	TX

To decipher, reverse procedures as they are described in Figures E and F. Letter pairs in the same row are substituted by the letters to the left; and letter pairs in the same column are substituted by the letters above. Decipher letter pairs in different columns with the third method (Figure G) which does not involve

C	A	L	I	F
O	R	N	B	D
E	G	H	K	M
P	Q	S	T	U
V	W	X	Y	Z

Figure E, first method: *The key word is CALIFORNIA.* If the two plaintext letters are in the same row, each is substituted by the letter to its right. If the plaintext letter is at the extreme right of the row, replace it with the first letter of that row. For example, QU would become SP, as color arrows indicate.

C	A	L	I	F
O	R	N	B	D
E	G	H	K	M
P	Q	S	T	U
V	W	X	Y	Z

Figure F, second method: If the two plaintext letters are in the same column, replace each with the letter below it. Substitute the bottom letter in the column with the letter at the top of that column. Following the chart above, IT is enciphered by BY.

C	A	L	I	F
O	R	N	B	D
E	G	H	K	M
P	Q	S	T	U
V	W	X	Y	Z

Figure G, third method: If the two plaintext letters are in different rows and columns, substitute each letter with the letters in the same row but in the column of the other letter of the pair. In our example, GB becomes KR.

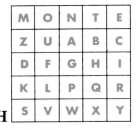

Figure H: Playfair Cipher using the key word MONTEZUMA.

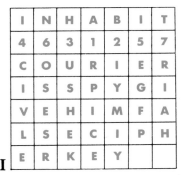

Figure I: In this Columnar Transposition cipher, letters of the key word INHABIT are numbered in the order they would be encountered in the alphabet. Thus A is 1, B is 2, and H, which would be the next letter encountered, is 3. Where letters repeat, as in I above, they are numbered consecutively. The plaintext message is written in rows under letters of the key word, as shown.

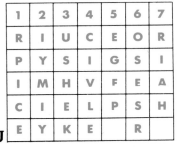

Figure J: For transmission of the Columnar Transposition message in Figure I, the numbers are written consecutively across the top. When the accompanying letters are entered in the rows below the numbers, the coded message appears.

reversing the enciphering procedure; each letter is deciphered by the letter in its row, but in the column of the other letter.

Problem 5:
Using the key word CALIFORNIA, encipher the following plaintext:

DO NO TA LX OW EN TR YT OA GE NT US IN GA LI AS ED UA RD OX

Problem 6:
With the same key word, decipher the following ciphertext:

OGIFI RCHAF SEGOP LLRTU LRMZQ PBOGO KFBRO GNWRN XL

Problem 7:
Using a 5 x 5 cipher square with the key word MONTEZUMA, as shown at left (Figure H) decipher the following ciphertext using the three methods discussed: (Note that the J is dropped.)

LU KE MT MO EI GR IT KY YG BQ IY WR EN IP GW IX

Columnar Transposition
Columnar transposition is simpler than the Playfair Cipher and much more easily broken. In the example at left (Figure I), INHABIT is the key word. The plaintext message, written to be read across the rows under the numbered key word is:

COURIER IS SPY GIVE HIM FALSE CIPHER KEY

The message is encoded by transposing the vertical columns into numerical order. To get the ciphertext, read down the transposed columns in figure J, from left to right, then write the letters in groups for transmitting:

RPICE IYMIY USHEK CIVLE EGFP OSESR RIAH

When this message is received, the recipient, knowing the key word to be INHABIT, writes it out with its number equivalents as in Figure I. He then writes letter group 1 of the ciphertext vertically under the number 1, group 2 under number 2, and so on, proceeding until the plaintext appears.

Problem 8:
Decipher this message using INHABIT as the key word:

Ciphertext: **BTETES LHCWM UNDCNT DGMTHN EAOIY OEAAEI ASNTU**

Now that you have tried to solve each of the cryptograms above, check your answers against those on the opposite page.

Toys and Games
Signal communications

Semaphore Flag Code: The history of military signal communications can be traced back to the ancient Greeks who used a system of fires in hollowed-out tree trunks for signaling to ships at sea. As early as the 16th century, a code based upon the number and position of signal flags had been developed for communication between naval vessels. During the 17th and 18th centuries, naval commanders improved upon and refined the system into one which is considered a forerunner of the Semaphore code as we know it today. In the position chart on the opposite page, notice that the letter positions A through I are also the positions for numbers 1 through 9. Zero equals the letter J. The signaler takes the numeral position before indicating a number he wishes to transmit. To indicate "error" or "attention", the signaler first takes the appropriate position then moves his flags in the directions indicated by arrows.

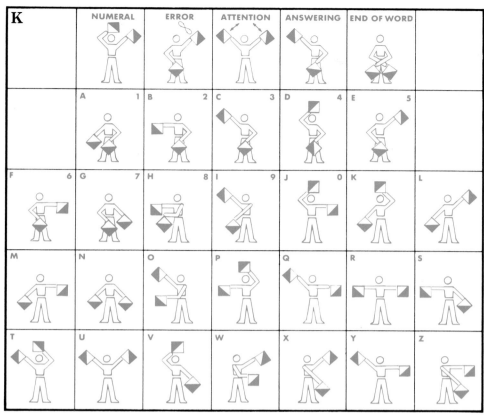

Figure K: The two-arm Semaphore code is used most often in naval communication and by Boy Scouts. Almost any visual signaling apparatus can be used, such as arms, flags or lights, if two are placed simultaneously in the correct positions.

Morse Code: The invention of telegraphy by Samuel Morse in 1832 revolutionized the communication sciences by introducing the possibility of using electrical impulses as signals that could travel at incredible speed over vast distances. Morse himself invented the famous code which is based on a simple alphabetic system of dots and dashes. Morse also devised a method for learning the code quickly, illustrated below. Each letter of the alphabet is assigned a word beginning with

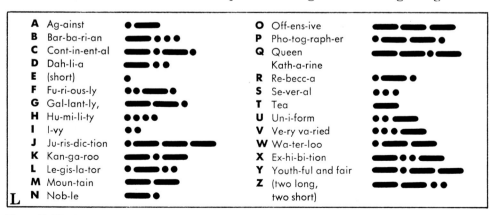

Figure L: The Morse code can be learned as quickly as the words above can be memorized.

that letter. The word breaks down into the same number of syllables as there are dots and dashes for that letter. Short and long syllables correspond to dots and dashes. The Morse code can also be used with flags, blinking lights and even whistle blasts. Try tapping out the first message ever sent (by Morse) over a telegraph: "What hath God wrought!"

Answers to cryptographic problems

1. RUSH REPLY
   mspr mokfx

2. LDSK XHKSU IDWG
   wait until dark

3. NTIPC GTIOG JATCP LSCMG TMN
   Send agent to headquarters.

4. CEEKT MNJII TEASI GHIGE TCPTM JONKX
   WHIG
   All personnel hunting leader of spy ring.

5. DO NO TA LX OW EN TR YT OA GE NT US
   or br if jq nl rv ho bq iy rc hg bs pt
   IN GA LI AS ED IA RD OX
   lb gr if jq no fq no nv

   Ciphertext in five-letter groups for transmission: ORBRI QNLRV HOBQI
   YRCHG BSPTL BQRIF LQMOF QNONV QNONO

6. OGIFI RCHAF SEGOP LLRTU LRMZO
   PBOGO KFBRO GWWRN XL

   Reliable ciphers can stand up under minor erxorsx.

7. Form enemy ciphers with cryptography.

8. Double agent has made contact with enemy units.

DECOUPAGE

Lustrous Cutouts

Marian Rubinstein studied decoupage at the Adventures in Crafts studio workshop in New York, where she works alongside her former teachers, Dee Davis and Dee Frenkel. In the shop, she sells a variety of decoupage materials and offers advice to decoupeurs, based on her very varied experience with decoupage pieces. Always involved in the arts, Marian was at one time a designer of canine fashions, for which she received prizes in New England shows.

Though the word decoupage is French, classic decoupage began in seventeenth-century Venice, where it was called *arte povero*, the poor man's art. Venetian cabinetmakers cut out and applied paper prints and reproductions to their cabinets, then coated them with varnish. The furniture that resulted looked as elegant as the two styles then in vogue with European aristocracy, furniture hand-painted by court artists and Chinese lacquerware furniture, but it was far less expensive. The popularity of decoupage spread rapidly through Europe and later to America. Today, decoupage is enjoying a renaissance: classic styles are revived; contemporary styles are being developed.

Translated from the French, decoupage means cutting up. The decoupeur selects prints, seals them to prevent the colors from running, and very carefully cuts them out. But first the surface to receive the decoupage must be prepared by sanding away imperfections. It is then given a coat of sealer and painted. When the surface is smooth and completely dry, the prints are applied to it with glue and are flattened down so that all portions of the prints adhere permanently.

The next, and most crucial, step is to bury the prints under many layers of clear lacquer or varnish. At certain points in the coating process, the surface is rubbed with wet sandpaper to level it. When the finish has been properly applied and leveled, your fingers cannot detect where the print area begins and ends.

Final steps include fitting the piece with hardware (if required), lining (if it is a box), and polishing with a fine paste wax to protect the piece from handling damage. Specific instructions for all these procedures are detailed in the Basic Techniques section, beginning on page 568.

The objects to be decorated can be purchased in a raw, unfinished state. Decoupage is also a good way to recycle discards and beautify barn-sale objects. The novice should begin by working with small objects, such as boxes, switch plates, lamps and cans on page 573, before moving on to larger and more complex pieces, such as furniture on page 577.

The surface most often decorated is wood. The Basic Techniques section deals with techniques relating to raw wood. Small variations of these techniques enable you to apply decoupage to finished wood, tin, ceramic, and stone. Instructions for preparing these surfaces are given in the Decoupage Craftnotes, page 569. Once you know the basic techniques and adaptations, you can experiment with still other materials.

Some of the sources for prints are pictured in the photograph at right. Sheets of prints made for decoupeurs are available at many craft and hobby shops. If your hobby shop does not sell them, the shop's manager may know of a manufacturer from whom they can be ordered.

As you will see in photograph 1, page 568, few specialized tools and materials are required for decoupage; many can be found in the home. The total cost of a project is reasonable and will seem quite low when compared with the prices of finished decoupage pieces offered by dealers.

Prints suitable for use in decoupage projects come from many sources, including gift-wrapping paper, magazine art, greeting cards, and foil trimming. In the foreground are prints made for decoupeurs. Applied to old furniture by decoupage techniques, prints such as these give the pieces a new look and a new appeal.

Basic decoupage techniques

The first step in the decoupage process is to prepare the base surface. The following directions are for unpainted wood objects. Directions for finished wood, tin, ceramic, and stone are given in Decoupage Craftnotes, page 569.

Sanding: First step in preparing the surface is to sand it. Photographs 2 and 3 show sanding procedures. When the piece is smoothly sanded, wipe it with a tack cloth to remove all particles of sawdust. This sticky cloth, a hardware-store item, is indispensable for keeping surfaces clean while you work. To preserve the tack cloth's stickiness, store it in an airtight container. Next step is to seal the surface to ready it for painting.

Sealing the Surface: Before you begin to work, seal raw wood. Three types of sealer are used: If the surface is to have a wood finish, stain, then seal with acrylic spray, or a brush-on liquid sealer. If the surface is to be painted, gesso, a white painting ground used by artists, is most often recommended, because it produces a porcelainlike surface that is a delight to work on. To apply acrylic spray, hold the can 10 inches from the object. Spray on two or three coats. Apply liquid sealer with a brush. Paint on two coats. Let dry between coats. Apply gesso as illustrated in photograph 4. After two coats of gesso have been applied, the object must be wet-sanded, following the directions for photograph 5. Wipe with the tack cloth after wet-sanding.

1: Basic tools and materials for projects in decoupage sold by art and craft supply shops include: oil pencils, in a variety of colors; bowl of water with small sponge; white glue; liquid sealer; sable brush (several sizes); sponge applicator; shears; tacking putty; manicure scissors; craft knife; burnisher; wooden stick; rubber rollers; wood block to wrap sandpaper around; ruler; tack cloth. In addition, you should have a piece of clear glass or mirror; spray-on acrylic sealer; a can of gesso; fast-drying acrylic paint; varnish or lacquer; fine paste wax (see specific details on page 571); steel wool; toothpicks; lint-free cloth.

Craftsman's tip: Experienced decoupeurs as a rule work on a number of projects simultaneously, as shown on these pages, so that while one project is drying they can be working on another.

2: To sand flat surfaces smooth, wrap fine-grade garnet sandpaper around a block of wood large enough to make broad strokes over the piece, yet small enough to fit comfortably in your hand. Always sand in the direction of the wood grain.

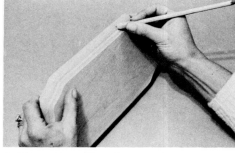

3: To sand small surfaces and hard-to-reach corners, wrap a piece of fine-grade garnet sandpaper around the eraser end of a pencil. This technique was used to sand the base of the lamp shown on page 573. Sand in the grain direction and dust.

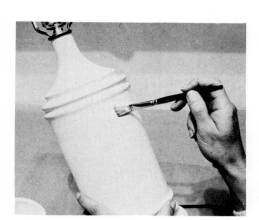

4: To seal with gesso, use a small brush or sponge applicator. Apply an even coat of gesso against the grain of the wood. When gesso is thoroughly dry, apply a second coat, brushing in the direction of the grain. Let dry.

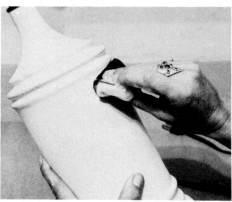

5: To wet sand after sealing with gesso, wrap No. 400 wet-or-dry sandpaper around a small sponge; dip in soapy, lukewarm water; then rub over gessoed surface in the grain direction. Let dry. Wipe up particles with a tack cloth.

6: If you are going to use paint on a gesso-sealed or a liquid-sealed piece, as here, paint should be applied in smooth strokes, from the center out to the edge. Avoid excess-paint build-up at the edges. Sand, with the grain, between coats.

7: To spray-seal prints with acrylic sealer, place the sheet of prints upright, and spray on two or three light coats. This will prevent the colors from running, make the paper firmer and easier to cut.

8: To cut straight edges of the print, place print on a pane of glass or mirror. Angle in the craft knife on the cutting line so that, when cut, the edge will be thinner than the rest of the print.

Painting: I use matte acrylic paint on all decoupage projects that require painting. It dries fast and looks good. Dip the brush halfway into the paint, and apply paint from the center of an area outward, as in photograph 6. After you refill the brush, make the next stroke away from the portion already painted; then work toward the wet edge. This is called feathering and is the secret of smooth painting. When paint is dry, apply a second coat. Then wet-sand lightly, with the grain, using No. 400 sandpaper. Wipe with the tack cloth. Paint on the third coat. Wait 12 hours. Then apply a coat of brush-on liquid sealer. This will keep the surface clean while you continue working.

Preparing the Prints: Once you have selected the prints you want to use, spray them with acrylic sealer to keep the colors from running (photograph 7). Then cut out the prints, as directed for photographs 8 and 9. Cut inside areas first so you have something to hold onto until the last bit is snipped. Examine the cut-out print for any white spots or borders. Use a moistened oil pencil to color these. Spray-seal the colored-in areas.

If you want to work with very old prints, first mount them either on thin cardboard or on book linen before cutting. If you are working with old prints that are foxed or water-stained, you can soak them in a solution of bleach and water. Remember that this is only for black and white engravings. The bleach would remove all colors from a color print.

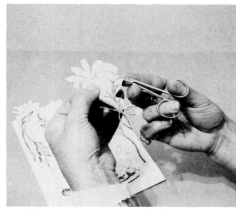

9. Hold manicure scissors with the thumb and ring finger, with the curved blades pointing away from print edge. This will give soft beveled edges. Support blades with index finger. Free hand must feed the print into the scissors.

10. Hold cut-out print securely and color any white edges with moistened oil pencil. Print should show no color breaks or edges. The colored-in areas must be spray-sealed before you decide to go on to the next step.

DECOUPAGE CRAFTNOTES

Preparing Additional Surfaces for Decoupage

Decoupage may be successfully applied to a great variety of surfaces. Each must be treated in a particular manner prior to gluing on the prints. Follow the instructions below for working with the most common surfaces.

Varnished or Waxed Furniture: Wash the surface with mineral spirits to avoid bleeding and adhesion problems.

New Tinware: Rinse the object in a solution of one part water and one part vinegar. Dry thoroughly. Then brush or spray on two coats of rust-resistant paint. When paint is dry, sand with fine-grade garnet sandpaper. Wipe with a tack cloth to remove sanding particles.

Old Tinware: Use heavy-duty steel wool to clean off all rust spots. Then follow instructions for new tinware.

Do not attempt to use decoupage on tinware that has a baked-enamel finish. Baked enamel will resist adhesion with paint, glue, and all finishes.

Stone: Scrub with soap and water; then dry thoroughly. Do not sand or seal. Prints may be applied directly to the unpainted stone, if you wish, and then varnished; or the stone can be painted first. Stone may also be lacquered.

Ceramic, Glazed or Unglazed: No special preparations are necessary. Simply make sure the entire surface is free of dust and grease.

Thinning Out Very Thick Prints

Prints should be as thin as possible before they are applied to a surface. Most of the prints suggested on pages 566 and 567 are thin enough to work with successfully. If you wish to use exceptionally thick, heavy postcard prints, or photographs, follow this method:

Seal front of the print with spray.

Coat wrong side with white glue, and let dry.

On the wrong side, peel up a corner. Place a pencil across it. Roll corner around the pencil until it is tight.

Keep rolling until the full layer of peeled-up paper is removed. The print should then be thin enough to use.

Rub the wrong side with fine sandpaper to smooth the surface and eliminate any thick spots.

Another method, requiring much more practice: Seal the print and soak it in vinegar and water. Then peel off the back.

11: To test composition, use tacking putty. This is especially important when working with rounded upright surfaces. Plan location of any hardware so that your arrangement does not interfere with it.

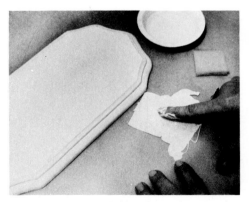

12: Apply water-soluble white glue evenly to the entire surface of the back of the print, using fingers, brush, or small sponge. Small flat surfaces are good beginner's pieces.

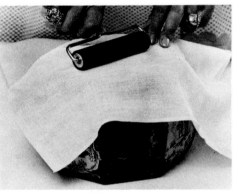

13: With print in position, covered with a lint-free cloth, roll gently to eliminate excess glue and air bubbles. Decorate one side at a time when working with boxes.

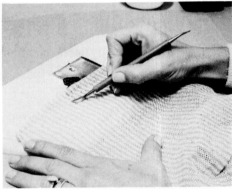

14: To burnish the edges of the print, work through a thin cloth, smoothing and flattening edges with the burnishing tool. With a toothpick, apply more glue to any edge that still sticks up.

Placing the Prints: Before you glue the prints down, test your design on the piece to be decorated. Use tacking putty, available in most hobby shops, to hold the prints as you work out the placement (see photograph 11).

Gluing Down Prints: Use white glue for permanent placement of the prints. Apply it to the back of a print as in photograph 12. Then, with your fingers or tweezers, put the print in place, and roll it as in photograph 13. If air bubbles are present, pierce them with a pin; then roll again. When all bumps are removed and the print is smooth and flat, burnish the edges (see photograph 14). Glue will be dry in minutes.

To glue down a very large print, first make a few discreet slashes across it with a craft knife. Try to make the slashes where natural lines occur in the print's design, so they will be less obvious. Then apply the glue. The slashes will let excess glue escape and will prevent a lumpy surface. With a very damp cloth, wipe off glue spots before you begin the embedding process.

This is the point at which some craftsmen sign their names to their pieces with paint or India ink. If your project is one that you want to sign, let the signature dry; then brush liquid sealer over it.

Embedding the Prints: This step is the most crucial one in decoupage. The clear finish chosen and the skill with which it is applied will determine the success or failure of the work. Three types of finish are available: water base (acrylic), lacquer, and varnish. Shellac won't last.

The water-base finish is synthetic. It dries quickly and is good for children's projects and for your projects if you are impatient. Many brands are sold; follow the manufacturer's directions carefully.

Lacquer is also fast drying. It produces a fine, high-gloss finish but is only recommended for pieces that will not be handled much. Flow on the lacquer with a brush. Do not go over any area you have just coated. Depending on the humidity, two or three coats can be applied each day. Each coat must be thoroughly dry before the next is applied. Continue coating until a thick, glasslike finish is achieved. Let the lacquered piece dry for 24 hours before handling it.

Clear gloss varnish is the most durable decoupage finish. Unfortunately, it is slow drying. Although the instructions on some varnish cans claim a six- to eight-hour drying time, I apply no more than one coat a day. Feather the varnish on, dipping your brush half-way into it, then stroking it on in the direction of the grain. To avoid creating air bubbles as you work, follow the suggestions given for photograph 15.

The day after the first coat of varnish is applied, dust with a tack cloth, and apply another coat. Add one coat a day until ten coats are applied. Then wet-sand as in photograph 5, page 568, using No. 400 or No. 600 sandpaper. When sanding over the print areas, you must level the finish without sanding into the print; easy does it. Whitish crumbs will fall off as you wet-sand. Don't panic; this is part of the process and is known as milking. When the surface feels smooth and even, check for small, shiny spots. These indicate areas missed in wet-sanding. Remove them with No. 0000 (very fine) steel wool. Then wipe the piece thoroughly with a tack cloth. Continue to coat with varnish—only one coat a day. Just how many coats you apply will depend on the appearance you wish to achieve and how deeply you want the prints to be embedded. You may wet-sand after every five or six coats of varnish, but this is not always desirable.

I usually stop coating with finish when I am no longer able to feel the edges of the prints and the piece has a deep, transparent finish. Whether you use water base, lacquer, or varnish as a finish, coat the undersides, insides, and all other areas of the piece with at least two coats. This will seal out moisture and prevent warping.

Waxing: With a lint-free cloth, rub on fine furniture paste wax or decoupage wax, following the directions for photograph 17. Never use spray-on furniture wax on decoupage pieces. It contains chemicals harmful to the decoupage finish and could eventually cause a mottled surface.

When the paste wax is dry, buff with a soft, dry cloth. Periodic waxing twice a year will protect your decoupage pieces from potential damage from moisture and handling.

Final Operations: Felt may be attached to the bottom of your piece with white glue. Use the glue sparingly, to prevent any excess that could spot the finish. Hardware, such as hinges, brass feet, clasps, and screws, should be attached with care, to prevent chipping nearby portions of the finish. If you wish to paint the hardware, do this before it is attached. Make sure any painted hardware is completely dry before you put it on.

Lining for Boxes: Boxes decorated with decoupage are usually lined. Lining materials include decorative paper and fabric. Two types of lining can be used: flat linings and soft, cushioned linings, which are padded, as illustrated on page 572. Both are glued to the inside walls of a box. To make a flat lining, use a ruler or tape measure to measure the inside dimensions of the sides and bottom of the box, and lid if there is one.

15: To apply finish, stroke it on with a sable brush, moving in the direction of the grain. When a small area is coated, draw the brush over it, against the grain, to remove air bubbles. Smooth the same section, this time with the grain.

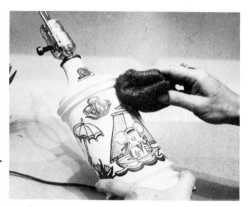

16: Rub the finished piece with steel wool if you want to give the surface a matte finish. Rub gently with the grain until the high gloss of the top coat of varnish is dulled. The lamp on page 573 was given a matte finish this way.

17. Wax the finished piece. Rub fine furniture paste wax sparingly on the object, using a slightly damp, lint-free cloth. Rub with a circular motion. When the wax is dry, buff the piece with a soft, dry cloth.

In measuring, try to be as precise as possible. Then cut paper or fabric to fit each of these surfaces. If the lining material is printed with a design, plan the patterned pieces of paper or fabric so that when they are cut and placed end to end, the design will match where they meet. Use white glue to attach the lining to the inside of the box. The lining's edges may be trimmed with glued-on ribbon or with gold foil.

To make a cushioned lining, measure the inside surfaces of the box as explained above. Cut pieces of heavy paper to these dimensions. Place the paper pieces on the lining fabric. Following the directions given for photograph 18, mark and cut out the fabric. Insert padding between fabric and pattern pieces (see photograph 19). Then carefully glue each cushioned piece into its place inside the box. Begin with the bottom piece; then glue on side pieces; end with the top piece (if the top has sides, end with the top side pieces). Trimming may be glued to exposed edges.

Tips

Once you have finished your first decoupage project, you will realize this is a simple, if time-consuming process. Use the tack cloth often to remove foreign particles from the surface of your piece. Work on a clean table, covered with brown paper, clear plastic, or aluminum foil. Newspaper would smudge your work; waxed paper might cause fisheyes, little spots of wax that would repel varnish. Keep tools and materials clean, and clear off work surfaces frequently. Avoid working near open windows; dust might fly in, and dust is the prime enemy when you are trying to create a smooth finish. Of course, always work with clean hands.

18: To prepare a cushioned lining for a box, measure and cut paper pieces to fit each inside wall, the lid, and the bottom. Place on the wrong side of lining fabric. Measure and draw a ¼-inch border around each piece. Cut along border.

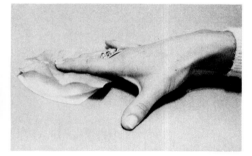

19: Three-layer cushioned lining consists of an even layer of cotton between lining fabric and its corresponding paper piece. Flip cushioned lining over, with fabric on bottom; cover paper surface with glue. Turn ¼-inch fabric border onto paper.

Recipe box, napkin holder, and wall file were a craftswoman's first projects. With the basic decoupage techniques, you can give new life to everyday objects like these.

Designs and Decorations
Mantel box, switch, lamp

The decoupage mantel box, switch plate, and lamp on this page were made following the basic techniques described on pages 568 to 572, with the few variations described below.

All three pieces were bought, unfinished, at a hobby shop. You can recycle similar pieces by decoupage as long as you prepare the surfaces as instructed on the preceding pages or in the Decoupage Craftnotes on page 569.

The designs shown, cut from gift-wrapping paper, are simply suggestions of what can be done with a little imagination. Don't try to find the same designs when you look for prints; use your imagination and ingenuity to vary the images and composition, so that the decoupage decorations are well suited to the objects you select.

Unless you are exceptionally patient, making one small piece at a time may be frustrating—the wait between coats is so long. Craftsmen usually work on several small projects simultaneously, beginning with one piece, and when it reaches the stage where it must be put aside to dry, starting a second. That is one reason we like to work on found objects like those on page 574.

Daisy Mantel Box

Sand the box, and apply brush-on liquid sealer. Apply three or four coats of acrylic paint. Note that the top daisy was composed with the box top closed. Cut the print and glue it on so the stem portion of the box top meets the stem portion on the box when the box is closed.

Varnish to a high gloss, using 15 to 25 coats of clear varnish; wet-sand after tenth to twelfth coats. If you have the patience to apply 25 coats, as I did, wet-sand again after the sixteenth and twentieth coats. Give the inside two or three coats of varnish to prevent warping.

Wax. Attach hardware, including brass ball feet and top hinge. Line with cushioned fabric and trim.

Switch Plate

You can apply decoupage to either metal or wood switch plates. If you are working with metal, rinse with a solution of one part vinegar and one part water; then apply a rust-resistant paint. Sand, and proceed to apply the decoupage exactly as though the metal were wood.

If you are working with wood, sand; seal with liquid sealer; paint. Paint screwheads for the switch plate, as these will show when the plate is mounted. Coat heavily with varnish (switch plates get heavy use); rub with steel wool; wax. Mount, making sure screwheads do not chip the finish.

Family-Room Lamp

The lamp base and shade at left were decorated with cutouts from the same sheet of gift-wrap paper. Sand the base, and then seal with gesso. Wet-sand until the surface is extremely smooth. Glue prints on carefully, as they tend to slip on a cylindrical surface while the glue is wet. Apply coats of clear gloss varnish until the prints are well buried in the finish. Wet-sand after the tenth coat. Then coat another 10 times, wet-sanding after the sixteenth. Rub with 0000 steel wool to produce a matte finish. Wax. Your final step is to glue felt to bottom.

The shade is made with an unusual technique, not described in the Basic Techniques section. After the prints are sealed with spray sealer, they are coated, front and back, with a decalling solution. This preparation is available in craft shops where decoupage supplies are sold; it is marketed under various trade names. The solution enables you to affix the prints to the shade without having to coat the entire shade with varnish. Follow the directions on the can. After the prints are in place, add velvet-ribbon trim, which may be handsewed or glued on.

June Crockett Smith is a founding member of the National Guild of Decoupeurs and teaches the art in her studio workshop in Corona Del Mar, California. She studied with Gene Clockman in Dallas.

Recycling household discards is both practical from an ecological point of view and challenging to the craftsperson. The decorative containers pictured below were made from tin cans that normally would have been thrown away.

Use cans with smooth surfaces and removable paper labels. Remove the label, and soak or sand off the glue strip. Then prepare the surface, following the directions for new tinware in the Decoupage Craftnotes, page 569. After applying rust-resistant paint, glue on the print. Use a small roller to flatten the print onto the can's curved surface. Use eight coats of clear gloss varnish. Wet-sand after the sixth. Add ribbon or foil trim.

The basic dimensions of the can on the far left in the photograph below were changed with a technique you can apply to other projects. A cardboard support was glued inside the top of the can so the print could extend above the edge of the can. Then yellow-green paint was dabbed onto the already painted can with a small sponge (see photograph 20). When the print was glued on, the green area became a grassy ground into which the print blended.

Cylindrical throwaway containers make inexpensive bases for decoupage work. These decorative pieces are, beneath paint and eight coats of varnish, just ordinary tin cans. When working on small projects, get several underway at once.

20: A yellow-green tone, dabbed onto the painted can with a small sponge, creates the impression of grassy ground, into which the print will blend. This is a trompe-l'oeil technique you can use for other projects.

Designs and Decorations
Tortoise-shell Base

To create the traditional tortoise-shell finish used as a background for the prints on the desk set at the right, you will need a few special materials: rottenstone powder, bronzing powder, asphaltum, and mineral spirits, sold in hardware and paint stores, plus glycerin and a drinking straw.

Prepare, seal, and paint the object to be decorated, following the directions in the Basic Techniques section, pages 568 to 570. Use gesso as the sealer and terra-cotta acrylic paint. Select and prepare prints. Black-and-whites look good with this finish, but you can use colored prints, too.

The antiquing substance used to create the finish is called mud. To make it, mix one part asphaltum, one part varnish, and one part mineral spirits. Place extra varnish and mineral spirits in individual containers and keep them near.

Photographs 21 to 24, page 576, detail the procedure that creates the tortoise-shell effect. Working on one surface at a time to avoid dripping, dab on mud. Then, with a scrap from a plastic dry-cleaning bag, drop varnish onto each dab of mud, and twist the plastic on the mud, as shown in photograph 22. With a pencil, flick bronzing powder over the stippled surface, as in photograph 23. Now dot the surface with drops of mineral spirits.

The surface will begin to flow as the materials react with one another. To make circular patterns, see photograph 24. To enlarge a circle opening, dip your finger in mineral spirits, and let a drop fall in the center of the

Desk set of black-and-white decoupage prints on a tortoise-shell ground has the look of heirloom pieces. The unusual technique that creates the tortoise-shell finish is explained in detail on these pages.

Detail of tortoise-shell finish shows the circular patterns that are created by blowing through a drinking straw onto a wet antiquing substance called mud.

21: To apply mud to the surface, make medium-size dots of it with a small paintbrush. Continue until the entire top of the box is dotted with mud. Work on only one surface at a time, or mud may get too dry for next step, stippling.

22: To stipple with varnish, use a wad of soft plastic from a dry-cleaning bag to drop varnish on each mud dot. Then twist the plastic wad over each dot of mud. Rewet the plastic with varnish whenever it becomes dry.

June applies varnish with a brush that is poked through the nipple section of a baby bottle to keep her hands clean. To clean the brush, she inserts it into a turpentine-filled baby bottle, tightens the cap, and moves the brush up and down.

23: To apply bronzing powder, hold a powder-covered pencil tip over the top of the box. With your fingers, flick the powder onto the surface until it is evenly speckled over the top. Next, drop mineral spirits over the entire surface.

24: The circular tortoise-shell motif is completed by blowing onto the flowing mixture through a drinking straw. The air blown through the straw makes mixture flow outward in a circle. Repeat this until you are satisfied with the pattern.

circle. Let dry overnight, or until you can tip the surface without causing the colors to run. Then repeat the process on each surface to be tortoise-shelled. When all are finished, let dry for 10 to 12 hours. Apply spray-on sealer and then a coat of varnish to set the colors. Let dry. Make a mixture of two parts white glue, two parts water, and one part glycerin. Using this mixture, glue the prepared prints in place. Secure by rolling and burnishing (see photographs 13 and 14, page 570). Let dry for 12 hours. Then apply up to 20 coats of clear varnish, one each day. When varnishing is completed, set the piece aside for five days.

Wet-sand, first with No. 400 sandpaper, then with No. 600. Wipe with a tack cloth. Then rub with No. 0000 steel wool, in the direction of the grain, until the piece assumes a dull appearance.

To polish, mix rottenstone powder with machine or mineral oil to make a paste. Apply paste with a wad of felt, and polish all surfaces. Clean away all traces of paste with fresh oil. Wax, as directed in the section on Basic Techniques, page 571.

Designs and Decorations
Decoupage cabinet

Many decoupeurs eventually try their hand at large pieces, because these offer the greatest challenge. It may take months to complete them. Before you attempt a project of such proportions, be sure you have mastered the basic techniques and have worked successfully on several smaller projects. Select prints appropriate for the period of the furniture piece to be decorated, and choose a finish suited to both the period and the print. Finish the piece, or, if already finished, prepare the surface as described in the Craftnotes.

The varnish cabinet below was first washed with mineral spirits. From that point on, the steps described in Basic Techniques were followed. Up to 40 coats of high-gloss varnish should be used over print designs of this size. Wet-sand after the tenth coat and after every seven coats from then on. After the last coat, polish with rottenstone powder and oil, as described on the opposite page. Then wax.

Details on how to finish fine furniture of the type here decorated with decoupage can be found in the entry "Finishing and Refinishing." For other related entries, see "Collages and Assemblages," "Framing," "Papercrafts," "Papier- and Cloth-Mache," and "Valentines."

An experienced decoupeur can create pieces of great elegance. This antique cabinet, decorated with exotic forest scenes, was further embellished with gold-foil trim. Instructions for applying decoupage to finished pieces appear in the Craftnotes.

DIORAMAS
Small Worlds

James Moran, left, and Vito Matti are president and vice-president of the New York Society of Model Engineers. Founded in 1926, the society is one of the oldest model-railroading clubs in the U.S. Members have built a diorama of a portion of the Pocono Mountains and have named their railroad the Union, Hoboken, and Overland.

A diorama is a miniature landscape or scene that looks realistic; it is wholly or partly three-dimensional. Diorama techniques are used to design window displays, to create landscapes around model-railroad tracks, to make three-dimensional school projects such as bonsai gardens, puppet stages, and historical scenes, and in dozens of other ways.

Following a few basic methods for modeling and painting, you can create any kind of diorama. These basic methods are explained in the directions for making a train diorama and a Scottish Highlands scene (page 583). Techniques for making landscapes, terrain, buildings, and human figures are described.

A model-railroad scene is one of the most popular kinds of diorama. The engine and trestle in the photograph below are part of a railroad layout built by the New York Society of Model Engineers. The track is 49 scale miles long and the model covers an area 45 by 12 feet. The landscape is constructed of plywood, pine boards, and wire-mesh screen covered with a pre-mixed modeling compound that creates the scenery, and the sky is painted.

This steam engine is a replica of a locomotive built during the early 1900s to haul ore cars. This—and the railroad dioramas that follow—are all drawn from a large layout built by the New York Society of Model Engineers.

Since a train diorama should look realistic, all parts of the scene must be made to the same scale. If in actual size a train is half as big as a building, then your model building should be twice the size of the model train in the diorama. Before designing the landscape and buildings, you must first choose the kind of model train you will use.

Two sizes are most popular among model railroaders. The scale called O gauge is about $1/48$th actual size. At this scale, the distance between the two rails is about 1¼ inches, and a 40-foot boxcar is represented by a model about 10 inches long. In HO gauge, about $1/87$th actual size, rails are about ⅝ inch apart, and a 40-foot boxcar is a model about 5½ inches long. This is the scale of the engine in the photograph on the opposite page.

The larger caboose is an O-gauge model, built on the scale of ¼ inch to the foot, $1/48$th actual size. The car in the foreground was built to HO scale, or $1/87$th actual size. Both cars are authentic in every detail.

A yard switcher engine rounds a curve near a rock cutting. Rocks are made of modeling compound and painted to look realistic. The warning light, wired to the tracks, is an automatic traffic signal used on this kind of blind hairpin curve.

In an area 4 by 8 feet, you can construct an HO layout with a landscape of hills and valleys. If space is more limited, you might use a midget-size model railroad such as the TT gauge, $1/10$ inch to a foot.

Locomotives and railroad cars (rolling stock) are replicas of actual trains. The wooden framework and cardboard sides of a passenger or freight car can be built from scratch; the wheels and undercarriage can be purchased at a railroad model supply store. Or the whole train, rolling stock as well as track components, can be bought in O, HO or TT gauge scale.

Track is spiked down to a permanent worktable called the track bench. The most convenient bench is a sheet of 3/4-inch plywood on top of sawhorses, low enough so that you can work sitting as well as standing. Most plywood comes in 4-by-8-foot sheets, large enough for an HO layout. For an O or larger setup, you can join plywood sheets with cleats. You can also use an old table, but keep in mind that you will damage the tabletop when painting, drilling, and driving nails for the diorama. Your track bench should be in as dry a location as possible, because moisture can damage the train layout.

It is important that you allow sufficient room so you can move all around your track bench. If you are working on quite a large layout, you might consider having holes (pop-ups) in the diorama, so that you can stand in them while you are working on otherwise hard-to-reach areas.

Laying Track

First, plan your layout, paying particular attention to the scale. A good start is to draw your layout outline on the table. You should plan straight and curved track, switches and crossovers. You can buy switches and crossovers at a model railroad supply store. With miniature rails, ties and spikes, you can lay your own track. We found the best materials are nickel-silver rail with fiber tie strips and steel spikes (photograph 1).

To lay straight track, begin by placing one section of tie strip against a secured piece of wood. Lay one rail in place along the ties. At every fourth tie, fasten the rail with two spikes, one on each side of the rail (photograph 2). Insert tacks with long-nose pliers and drive in with a tack hammer. Now lay the second rail, checking the distance from the first rail with the track gauge (photograph 3).

To lay curved rail, cut scrap wood to outside radius of desired curve, nail this down, lay tie strip against back-up piece as in figure A, and spike down rails. Be sure that your curve is not too sharp for the train.

1: Track-laying equipment includes lengths of nickel-silver rail (left), a coil of fiber tie strip (top), a track gauge (right), a box of miniature spikes. In the tie strips, ties are held together by connectors and holes are predrilled.

2: Start the spikes with a pair of long-nose pliers and drive home with a tack hammer. When one length of rail is in place, spike down a second rail. Holes in tie strip are slightly larger than spikes.

3: Use the track gauge to control spacing of rails. It should fit snugly between the rails. Hold it at right angles to the track. Check distance between rails by sliding the gauge along their tops.

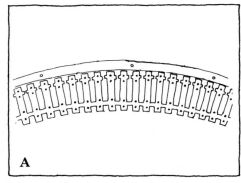

A

Figure A: On curves, lay tie strip as shown. Then lay outer rail in place, and spike down at every fourth tie. Remove back-up piece. Using track gauge as before, lay inside rail and spike it down.

It is important that all structures are in correct scale as they are in this scene.

Making a Tunnel

Where tracks enter a tunnel, the facades (portals) are modeled carefully to resemble an actual railroad scene. Cut supporting arches for tunnel from a sheet of ¼-inch plywood, nail these vertical sections to the top of the bench and cover as in figure B. Cut the tunnel portal that you will glue to the face of the arch from a piece of soft pine, scribe it with a razor knife, and paint to simulate stonework or brickwork. Glue it in place around the roadbed, tack down window screen to form a foundation for embankments.

Cover the tunnel and embankments with a pre-mixed modeling compound that you can buy in hobby stores. The compound is spread over the screen, as in photograph 4. In some instances you might wish to use foil or foamed plastic instead of screen as a base. This is optional.

4: Form embankments with wire screen. Tack the screen alongside the tracks, near the edge of the gravel roadbed. Press modeling compound into wire mesh.

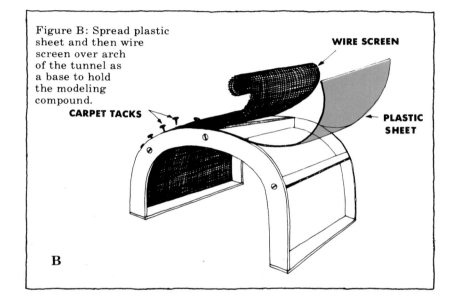

Figure B: Spread plastic sheet and then wire screen over arch of the tunnel as a base to hold the modeling compound.

WIRE SCREEN

CARPET TACKS

PLASTIC SHEET

B

5: Using modeling compound, cover edges of the tunnel portal. Make the portal of soft wood that can be carved with a knife to simulate a rock wall. Paint the interior of the tunnel black.

Tunnels with imitation-stone portals and wing walls, located in a mountainous section of the diorama.

Earthworks and Landscape

To create your landscape, build the hills and mountains in stages. On top of the bench, nail wood frames to give the contours of peaks and valleys. Tack window screen over the wood to make a foundation for the terrain; cover the screen with modeling compound, let it dry, and then paint (photograph 8).

You can add all kinds of buildings and natural features to the surface of the landscape. Make use of discards you find around your house or objects from outdoors. Look for new ideas in railroad books at the public library.

To make trees, gather dry twigs that have several branches (see photograph 6). From a hobby store, you can obtain lichen. Stores sell it dyed a limited range of colors, but you can vary the color with fabric dyes. Place white glue on the twig branches, and add lichen until trees look real (photograph 7).

Paint the landscape with several coats of artist's oil color, diluted with thinner (photograph 8). Where the ground is smooth, landscape colors should be painted shades of green and brown to simulate grass and earth. Rougher areas, such as rock cuttings, are painted shades of gray. Heavy shadowing helps emphasize the contour of rocks and stones.

When the paint is dry, add bushes around stone outcroppings and building foundations. The bushes here are small pieces of real sponge, dyed to natural colors, then glued onto the landscape in clusters (photograph 9).

On an HO scale, landscape features can be built from simple materials. Wood abutments can be made from popsicle sticks or tongue depressors. A station house, switch house, or terminal building can be constructed from basswood or cardboard braced at the corners with tape. Human figures can be made from twisted wire, steel wool, and mache, as explained on page 588.

6: Keep a supply of twigs on hand for making miniature trees for the landscape. Choose dry twigs with branches. Best are 2 to 3 inches in height for HO gauge.

7: Holding a twig upright, glue several pieces of lichen to the branches. Made in this way, the trees appear to be deciduous ones in leaf.

8: To give authenticity to the scene, apply several layers of artist's oil paint to the landscape. Proper colors and shading give a natural appearance.

9: Bits of sponge rubber are touched with white glue and placed near a roadbed. These simulated bushes can help cover any bare spots in the terrain.

This cement plant is located at a railroad siding and is serviced by a number of hopper cars and auxiliary work vehicles. The main building is made of basswood.

An industrial switcher of the saddle-tank type operates near the plant. It was built from a model kit and painted by hand. Engine and factory have been touched up realistically with paint the color of dust, mud, and rust.

In the distance are the Pocono Mountains, with forests and limestone cliffs. A blue sky, paler near the horizon, is painted on a curved screen. This background gives the illusion of being a natural skyline.

Carving and Molding
Portable diorama

$ ● 🚶 🎨

To make the Scottish Highlands scene below, a small, portable diorama is constructed on a plywood base. This type of diorama has a curved background and is lighted by an aquarium lamp above the frame (see photograph 29, page 591). Unlike the landscape around a model railroad, this scene is viewed through a limited opening (aperture) at the front of the diorama (the proscenium). The viewer has the impression that hills and sky are in the far distance while the figures, pond, stream, and cottage are nearby.

The way you design such a diorama accentuates this feeling of perspective. When making the background, you bend it into the shape of an elongated curve. As you look into the diorama, this elongation deceives the eye, and the depth appears to be greater than it actually is. Since the aperture limits the scene within a single frame, the horizon at the sides of the background seems to be as far away as the horizon in the rear.

Landscape, cottage, and figure in the foreground are all standing objects. By modeling these as lifelike, three-dimensional features against a two-dimensional background, you increase the scene's naturalness. With matching coloration, the background seems to be a continuation of the landscape.

George Crawbuck, a senior preparator at the American Museum of Natural History, helped reconstruct a dinosaur skeleton that was sent to Japan for an exhibition, and he designed the plastic figures of Tyrannosaurus rex and Neanderthal man that were reproduced by a toy company. He has taught adult courses in making dioramas.

This diorama portrays a Scottish Highlands scene in the year 1745. A young Scottish soldier, dressed for battle, waves farewell to his father. The old man, a Highlands farmer (crofter), is standing in front of his stone cottage. House, figures, and landscape details in the foreground are three-dimensional.

10: To form the contour of the landscape, tack wire screen over blocks of wood. The size of the blocks and their location in the diorama are shown in figure D. When the screen is in place, trim the outer edges to match the perimeter.

Background and Landscape

A sketch for the background view is given in figure C. Transfer this pattern to a single sheet of heavy, two-ply cardboard, purchased at an art-supply store. Lay the cardboard on a flat surface. Use a razor knife to cut the cardboard to the dimensions given in figure C. Be sure to cut notches in the upper right and upper left corners. Following figure C, sketch the outlines of landscape, hills, and horizon on the cardboard.

To color the background as shown in photograph 11, use acrylic paints thinned with water. Paint the top of the cardboard blue. Distant hills at the sides are edged with a darker shade of blue. The low horizon in the center and clouds are light gray or white. The foreground hills are painted green.

The base of the diorama, shown in figure D, starts with a piece of ¾-inch plywood 21 inches wide and 14½ inches deep. On the smoothest side of the board, trace a semicircle to mark the position of the background. The center of the curve (marked with a cross in figure D) is 3 inches in from the front edge of the board, to give the desired perspective effect, and the radius is 9 inches. Tie a pencil to the end of a string; measure off 9 inches, and pin down the string at the center point. Then swing the pencil in an arc to draw the semicircle. Blocks of wood around the edge will hold the background (photograph 15) in place. To make a foundation for the landscape, nail down wooden blocks of various heights (see photograph 10 and figure D). Over the blocks, tack down pieces of window screen to create the flowing contours of the landscape. With a pair of wire cutters, trim the perimeter of the screen to fit exactly against the curve of the background.

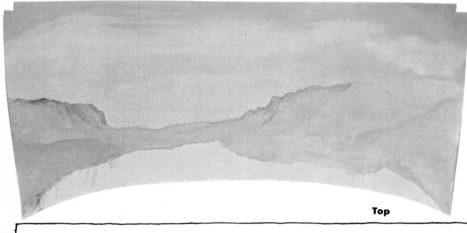

11: Paint hills and skyline on a cardboard background. At the base of the cardboard is a blank area that will be hidden by the landscape; leave this area unpainted. Color low, nearby hills shades of green. Soften the mountains in the distance with deep blue and some lighter tones to give the impression of low clouds and mist.

▼ Figure C: Using the pattern shown here, cut the background from a single sheet of heavy, two-ply cardboard. Cut notches at top for a proscenium brace. With a pencil, lightly sketch hills, landscape, and horizon on the cardboard.

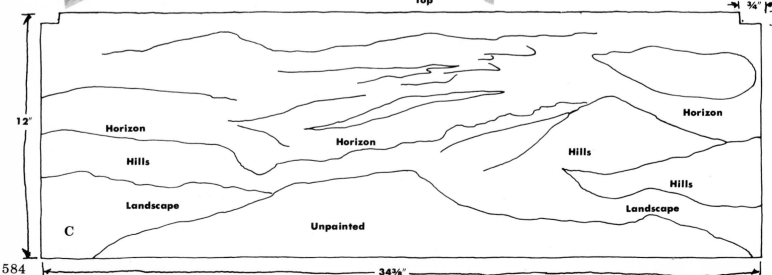

Top

¾"

½"

12"

Horizon

Horizon

Horizon

Hills

Hills

Hills

Landscape

Landscape

Unpainted

C

34⅜"

To make a three-dimensional landscape surface, wire screen is covered with soft mache. I make my own mache by thoroughly mixing one part sifted dextrin (dry glue), two parts powdered asbestos, three parts plaster of Paris (you can purchase at paint store), adding water gradually until the mixture is workable (photographs 12 and 13). Apply it to the wire screen, pressing down firmly with a putty knife or trowel (photograph 14). It's a good idea to work with a solid particle mask, which you can also get at the paint store. Or, you may wish to try one of the pre-mixed modeling compounds, which you can buy at hobby stores.

Make a brace from three strips of wood (figure D). The uprights are ¾-inch square, and the crosspiece is ¾ inch by ½ inch. Cut two of the uprights (10¾ inches), and nail to the crosspiece (19½ inches). On the base, nail wooden blocks to hold the foot of the brace, as shown in photograph 15. Check fit of brace to background and put aside until final assembly (page 591).

12: Materials needed for mache are one part sifted dextrin (dry glue), two parts powdered asbestos, three parts plaster of Paris. Mix these dry ingredients before adding water. It sets quickly.

13: To mix mache, add water gradually to dextrin, asbestos, and plaster of Paris. Stir with a trowel until all the dry ingredients have been blended thoroughly to a puttylike consistency.

14: At the perimeter of the screen, stand up a piece of curved cardboard, 5 inches high, as a stand-in for the background. Then, beginning at the perimeter, spread plaster mixture over wire screen.

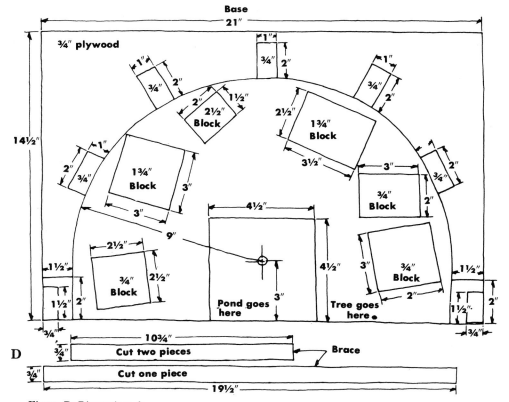

Figure D: Dimensions for base and brace.

15: Brace fits around opening of diorama. It is not put on until final assembly.

Landscape Features

Mache is a very hard material when it dries, so most of the landscape features should be added while the surface is still moist. However, do not landscape the area around the center until you have made the pond.

The construction of the pond is shown in figure E. To simulate water, cut out a piece of blue paper 4½ inches square, and glue it to the plywood base. Cover paper with a sheet of ⅛-inch clear plastic. Over the plastic, place a wire screen with a 3½-inch-diameter hole cut in it. Center the hole over the blue paper. Screen should extend beyond the square edges of the plastic.

Other features of the landscape include a stream, a path, sand, stones, long and short grass, heather, and a single tree. Mold the stream bed in mache, and smooth the bottom with a wet brush. Paint the bottom light blue, and simulate foam in the stream bed by overlaying the surface with glue.

Since there is glue in the mache, it serves as an adhesive as well as a covering. Sprinkle sand around the edge of the stream bed on the wet mache, and blow away the excess that does not stick. To make a path, mix glue with dry sand, and spread the mixture over dry mache. Adding glue to the surface makes it appear damp or muddy. Gather a number of small stones, and scrub them clean with a brush and water. Set aside to dry. When the pond is in place, place these stones near the bank, as shown in photograph 17.

Cover screen around pond with wet mache, and press in a clump of dry flax at one side (photograph 18). When stones and long grass have been placed, smooth the edge of the pond with a wet brush (photograph 19). A branch serves as a tree trunk. Bore a hole in the diorama base, and whittle the branch end to fit it snugly. Glue lichen to the branch for foliage (page 582).

16: Materials for making the landscape features include (counter-clockwise) sifting screen, clean stones, flax, branch, and dried lichen. Jars contain plain, uncolored flock, flock mixed with green dry color, and sand.

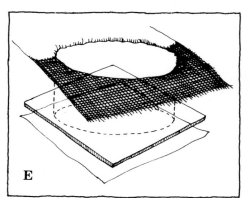

E

Figure E: To make the pond, lay a sheet of clear plastic over a blue-paper square. Cut a hole 3½ inches in diameter in a wire screen, and lay the screen over the plastic. Cover the screen with mache.

17: Before mache has dried, press scrubbed stones into the soft shoreline at the edge of the pond. Now carefully brush shellac over the base of the stones to make them appear wet.

18: With a pair of tweezers, insert a clump of flax into soft mache. Broom straws, reeds, or corn tassels may be used if flax is not available. Finally, apply shellac to stalks.

19: Smooth the mache with a wet brush. For a pebbly or stony landscape, let the mache dry while it is still rough. Surface cannot be smoothed once it has dried, for mache is very hard when dry.

Much of the Scottish Highlands is barren and windy, but parts of the ground may be covered with heather, grass, and mosses all year round.

20: For a grassy look, first use an old paintbrush to spread flat varnish over a layer of sand. This should be done only when the mache is completely dry.

21: Next, sift the flock through a wire screen, and spread it evenly over the wet varnish. Colors should resemble the nearby hills painted on the background.

Short grass, in a diorama of this size, is no more than a thin, fluffy covering of flock that has been dyed various shades of green. If you want to make your own colors, purchase undyed flock and dry colors from a hobby store. Put a small amount of a green dry color in a jar, and add flock until the jar is loosely filled. Shake briskly until all the flock is covered with the powder. By varying the proportions of dry color and mixing in darker and lighter colors, you can simulate colors of weeds, ferns, and moss.

To glue down the flock, spread flat varnish over the surface of dry mache with an old paintbrush, as shown in photograph 20. Pour the flock onto a wire-mesh screen, and sift it over the landscape until it is spread evenly (photograph 21). When varnish is dry, blow away the excess flock and powder.

Grass and sand should cover the visible areas of the scenery. Be sure to extend these features all the way to the back (curved) edge of the landscape and all the way to the front of the diorama. If any chipped or bare areas of mache are still showing, they can be touched up with varnish and covered with flock.

To make the features around the water appear wet, brush shellac on the stems of reeds and the bases of stones near the stream and pond.

Lichen, which makes realistic bushes, can be purchased in several colors at hobby stores. Glue the lichen to the shoreline and ridges of the landscape, as shown in photographs 22 and 23. Bushes will also help in covering bare spots of mache.

22: For bushes, apply a small amount of white glue to dry green lichen. Norwegian lichen simulates Scottish heather and retains its green color when dry.

There are many items that can be used to imitate grass and bushes, and you should be able to find some of these substitutes around your home. Packing straw or excelsior, used to protect pieces of china, can be cut in bunches for long grass. For weeds and moss, you can use lint that comes from a clothesdryer. Be sure to sift it two or three times, until it is broken up into fine pieces. Bushes can be made from ball cotton or pieces of sponge.

It is not advisable to use organic materials, such as flowers or leaves or live grass, in a diorama. Unless they are carefully preserved, they change color and become brittle in a very short time.

23: Press lichen onto the dry surface of mache, and allow it to spring back into shape. Place bushes along the ridge and near the stream bed.

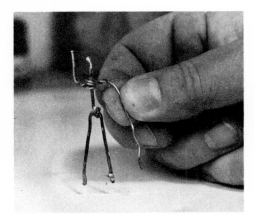

24: A stick figure of the old man is shaped from pieces of wire. Using pliers, wind the pieces tightly at the neck and waist. With a wire cutter, trim the arms, legs, and walking stick. A single wire forms arms and stick.

25: Wrap picture wire around layers of steel wool to flesh out the skeleton of the figure. Mache cannot be applied to bare wire, but it adheres to steel wool. The walking stick may be left bare and painted brown.

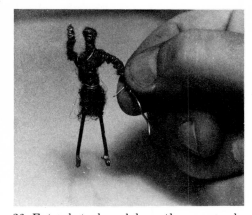

26: Extend steel wool down the arms and legs of the wire figure. Leave the ends of the leg wires bare so they can be planted in mache. To make a knotty stick, twist the wire in several places, and paint the knots dark brown or black.

The soldier in the foreground carries a targe (shield), which is actually the size of a penny. Studs on the targe are made from pinheads, clipped off with wire cutters.

Making a Figure

Although plastic and metal figures can be bought at hobby stores, you can make a realistic model with very few materials. The figures in the Scottish Highlands scene are about 2 inches tall.

To make a skeleton, twist 14-gauge wire into the shape of a stick figure. Using pliers, form wire into a V shape for the legs. Then wrap another wire around the point of the V, and extend it to become the torso and head. Finally, wrap another piece of wire around the torso, and extend it to form arms, shoulders, and cane (see photograph 24).

Since mache will not adhere to the bare wire, cover the surface with steel wool, wound several times with picture wire, as shown in photograph 25. When the figure is ready to be covered with mache (photograph 26), twist the legs, arms, and torso into their final shape. The bottom tips of the wire legs and cane should not be covered with steel wool; these points go into the mache (ground) when the figure is in position.

Mix the dry materials for mache according to the proportions used previously (page 585). Add water until the mixture is the consistency of modeling clay. It should adhere to the steel wool but be easy to model.

Cover the steel wool with mache, as shown in photograph 27. The features of the face, such as beard and brows, should be sculpted while the mache is still wet. Use a pin or razor knife for fine details.

When the mache is dry, add clothing and accessories to the figures. Both the old man and the soldier are wearing kilts and cloaks. These are made from tissue paper dipped in glue and draped on the figures while the glue is still wet (photograph 28). The old man's sporran (pouch) is a painted piece of cardboard. To make the soldier's targe (shield), trace around a penny on a sheet of thin cardboard; cut out the circle, and glue it to the soldier's arm. His bonnet is made of paper, with a strip of tissue for a feather.

Use oil colors for painting the figures. Paint flesh tones and light colors first, then the jackets and tartan patterns.

The Crofter's Cottage

The cottage is made of pieces of ⅛-inch-thick cardboard. Sides are painted to resemble stonework, and the roof is covered with simulated thatching. Stones on the roof are a typical feature of a crofter's hut; in the Scottish Highlands, the stones prevent strong winds from blowing away the light thatch.

Cut out sections of the cottage according to the patterns, figure F. Make two each of the chimney piece, the front and back wall, and the roof section. Dotted lines in the sketch indicate where the roof sections should be folded. Before folding, score the cardboard with the point of a compass or the edge of a dull knife. Then turn over the cardboard, and fold the flaps upward at right angles: the creases should be straight and without wrinkles.

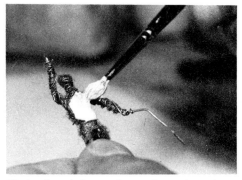

27: Apply mache to the surface of steel wool with a small brush. Use several layers to model limbs and features; then smooth with a wet brush. Make sure the wires are in the desired position before applying mache.

28: To make a cloak (scarf), drape one shoulder with a piece of tissue dipped in glue. The cloak is wrapped across the chest and falls behind the knees in back. For tartan, paint the cloak red, and crisscross with black stripes.

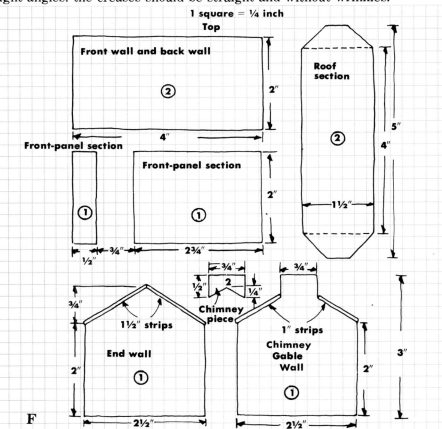

Figure F: Using these patterns, cut out sections of the crofter's cottage from ⅛-inch (No. 30) cardboard. Circled numbers indicate how many pieces of each section you should cut. The dotted lines indicate folds.

To assemble the cottage, glue chimney pieces on the inside of the gable, as shown in figure G. Make the front wall a double thickness by gluing the front-wall piece behind the front-panel sections, to create a door recess. Glue the end walls to the edges of the side walls. With masking tape, secure the outside corners to hold them until the glue sets. Apply glue to tabs on the roof sections, fold tabs down, and slide the roof sections into place. Cut strips to cover the joints between roof and end walls, figure G.

Since two sides of the cottage are not visible, only two need be finished. Paint the inside of the doorway black. Then, with watercolors, paint the sides of the cottage to resemble masonry. First, apply a wash of basic gray to the front panel and gable end. Make highlights with short, vertical streaks of white; with black, paint dark horizontal shadows to resemble the undersides of stones. Dark brown and light gray vary the stone colors. When sides are painted, cover the roof with a thatching of flax or broom straws and glue small stones along the eaves.

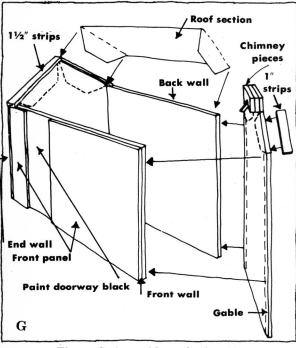

Figure G: Assemble crofter's cottage as shown. Score and fold roof sections. Back up front-panel sections with the front-wall section.

Assembly

You are now ready to assemble the diorama. Following the dimensions in figure H (below) make the proscenium out of pressboard. The steps are simple; just make sure that you have studied the diagram well before you start cutting. Now cut out the aperture. Just below it drill holes for the screws.

To position the old man and his son, drill holes for their feet with an ⅛-inch wood drill. Touch glue to the bare ends of the wires, and insert them into holes in the mache.

Glue the cottage to the landscape near the perimeter. Camouflage the foundation of it with sand and flock. In this way you will have achieved the feeling of naturalness, as though the cottage had been there for a long time.

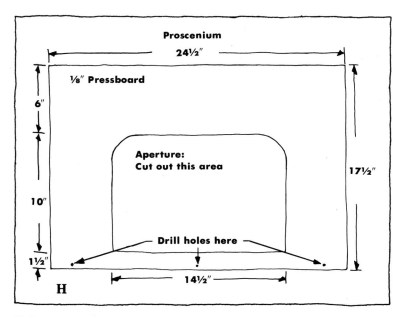

Figure H: Pattern for proscenium. Trim pressboard to size. Drill a ¼-inch hole in one corner of aperture and use a coping saw to cut out area in the center. Along the bottom, drill three ⅛-inch holes for screws: holes should be centered ½ inch from the bottom of the proscenium.

Bend the cardboard background until it fits snugly in front of the wooden blocks, as shown in the photograph below. Any burrs along the edge of the mache can be removed with either a putty knife or a rasp.

In order to hold the edge of the background upright, you can place the brace, which you have already made (page 585), over the opening, as shown in photograph 15, page 585.

The next step is to attach the proscenium to the front of the diorama in order to frame the scene. Use ½-inch wood screws to attach it to the edge of the plywood base. It should not be attached to the wooden brace.

When looked at from above, the diorama should now appear as in the photograph below. The proscenium hides the brace, the edges of the background, and the base of the diorama. The background fits tightly against mache at the perimeter, and so there are no visible cracks between the foreground and the background.

It is important to remember that mache sets quickly and therefore you should mix only a small amount at a time. If you find you don't have enough, simply mix more.

Viewed now from the front, the elongated curve of the diorama gives the impression of a greater depth than there actually is. The scene is within a single frame and so the horizon at the sides of the background seems to be as distant as the horizon at the rear.

To light the diorama, rest a 20-inch aquarium lamp on top of the background as shown in photograph 29.

For related projects, see the entries "Bonsai," "Boxes," "Carving," "Dried Flowers," "Papier- and Cloth-Mache," "Wildlife," and "Woodworking."

29: Use a 20-inch aquarium lamp for scenery lighting. This kind of lamp is very lightweight and can be supported by the edges of the cardboard.

Attached to the front of the diorama, the proscenium screens from view the edges of cardboard and plywood and the brace. Viewed from above, as here, the background appears slightly parabolic in shape. This curve gives the viewer the best illusion of distance and provides a non-reflecting surface when lighted. Background, brace, and proscenium can be removed easily for cleaning the diorama or for touching up the surface features.

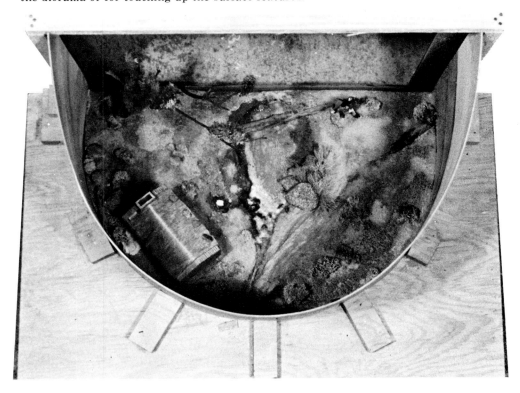

DOLLHOUSES AND FURNITURE
Living Little

Margaret Perry is Travel and Craft Editor of Early American Life *magazine. Her travels have taken her far from her native Connecticut in her search for historic sites and early crafts, both here and abroad. She is the author of* Christmas Magic, Rainy Day Magic, *and* Christmas Card Magic.

A dollhouse, whether it costs pennies or a fortune, has the fascination of all miniature things. There is something irresistible, to adults as well as to children, in tiny rooms inhabited by Thumbellina people and fitted out with furniture made to scale. For play, children often prefer the expendable type of dollhouse pictured on pages 594 and 595, made, with their help, of cardboard and household discards. But they usually are fascinated by antique dollhouses like the pink one shown below, which belongs to FAO Schwarz, a famous New York toy store.

Some of the most famous dollhouses have been owned by Hollywood film stars. The one that belonged to Colleen Moore, silent-movie star of the 1920s, has floors covered with jade, mother-of-pearl and quartz. It has been exhibited around the world to raise funds for charities, and it is now permanently on display at the Museum of Science and Industry, Chicago. Za Su Pitts' dollhouse, shown opposite, is in the Shelburne Museum, Inc., Shelburne, Vt. Museum dollhouses usually are architecturally authentic and are furnished with miniature pieces representative of the period when the houses were built.

▶Antique English dollhouse is more than a hundred years old. It has glass windows, and a hinged front that opens to show the interior. See page 600 through 603 for instructions on making a similar dollhouse.

European dollhouses of past centuries, sometimes made and furnished in exquisite detail, were given to little girls to help them learn the proper running of a household.

Not all wooden dollhouses are museum items, of course. Some are made for children to play with, some for displaying private collections of miniatures. The pink house pictured opposite could serve either purpose. Instructions for making it are given on pages 600 through 603. To complete such a house requires patience, time and some knowledge of woodworking. You may enjoy improving on the materials suggested: a fireplace of stone chips and more intricate gingerbread trim on the roof would be fun to improvise. The corrugated cardboard roofing suggested is another improvement. The original is constructed of wood painted to look like old brick, with white trim. All windows, except one that was damaged and is now cellophane, are glass.

Dollhouse People and Furnishings

On pages 598 and 599 are instructions for making dollhouse people of cloth, with wire frames and, on pages 596 and 597, for making some basic furniture. You can make these pieces much more elaborate—for example, cover the little chairs with petit point rather than scrap cloth; or make a minute sampler for a wall, a small lacy cloth for a table. The tiny deck of cards, on page 596 is one of my favorite miniatures. Once you start furnishing a dollhouse, delightful possibilities for miniaturization will occur to you.

Museum shops, antique shops, and variety stores are likely places to look for small furnishings that would be difficult to make—dishes of china, pewter, copper kitchenware, and glass vases, for instance.

ZaSu Pitts' dollhouse, named "Ramshackel Inn", after a play in which she appeared, is in the permanent collection of the Shelburne Museum, Shelburne, Vt.

This English dollhouse, also in the Shelburne Museum, displays a charming collection of miniature furnishings.

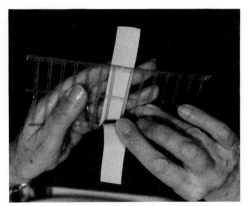

1: Attach details, such as dollhouse porch railing cut from a plastic berry basket, with tape of the same color.

Simple, expendable dollhouses that stand a lot of wear can be made of cardboard cartons or posterboard, and decorated with paint, self-adhesive vinyl, contact paper or wallpaper. The basic materials and equipment you need are: posterboard or cartons of various sizes; artist's or mat knife for cutting; epoxy glue; sheets of self-adhesive vinyl or contact paper; felt pen for drawn details; self-sticking plastic tape to affix lightweight parts; cellophane strapping tape to hinge collapsible dollhouses; colored plastic tape to finish raw edges; quick-drying enamel paints. The other materials used are discards, such as leftover wallpaper, bits of felt and fabric, cardboard tubing, and plastic berry baskets.

To make the four-room house (see photo below and Figure A3 opposite), glue together two small cartons for the dining room and kitchen. Next, cut off corners of larger cartons for the living room and nursery. Use cardboard strips for roofing over the porch and over the cut-off carton sections. Glue room assemblies together. Cover exterior sides and back with self-adhesive contact or vinyl resembling wood, and paint roof areas dark green.

With the rooms assembled, I searched for materials to create appropriate details. The living room balcony (painted) and porch railings (unpainted) are from a cut-up berry basket. Pillars supporting the porch roof are 1-inch wide, stiff cardboard strips. The living room door is a 2½ by 5½-inch strip of paper, glued to the wall and marked with a felt pen to look paneled. Doors and windows can be cut out or drawn on. The interior walls are covered with scraps of contact paper or wallpaper, and the porch floor with dark-green felt.

The simple fold-up doll rooms opposite were made in similar fashion, using medium weight cardboard or posterboard, and hinging walls as in figure A.

Four-room dollhouse has a kitchen and dining room, made of two small cartons, and a living room and nursery made of larger cartons. Slanted rooflines are created by cutting away carton corners. Carton edges have been finished with colorful plastic tape. A layout for this dollhouse is given in figure A3, on the opposite page.

Above: Two-wall doll room is
made as shown in figure A1.
Below: Three-wall room is made as
in figure A2. Floor is carpeted with
a single layer of green felt.

2: With room walls hinged as shown at
right, cover interior walls with vinyl or
contact paper that overlaps to exterior,
and then cover exterior walls with paper
patterned to look like wood, as shown
above. Apply this self-sticking paper
with the walls spread out flat as shown.
The strapping tape and the lapped-over
border of the interior wall covering will
be hidden under the exterior wall covering.
The same techniques used for cutting,
hinging and decorating a two-wall room
can be used for the three-wall rooms
shown at left and below.

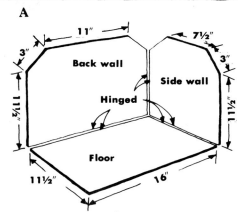

Figure A1: Two-wall room: run strapping
tape along full length of hinged walls.

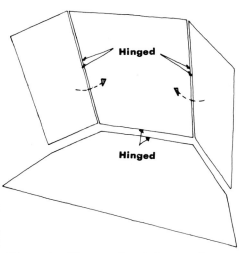

Figure A2: Hinge walls of three-wall room
with tape as shown. Rectangular room
(left, below) is made the same way.

Three-wall rectangular doll room is also hinged as in figure A2, so that it
can be folded and stored flat. Walls and floor are cut, hinged, and covered
with vinyl or contact paper in the same way a two-wall room is, as described
in the caption for photograph 2.

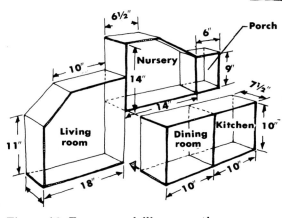

Figure A3: Four-room dollhouse on the
opposite page is assembled in sections
as shown; sections are glued together.

595

The lure of the miniature led me to make these playing cards. They are a single piece of stiff paper, with edges and characters drawn on with colored felt pens. The overall size of the cards is ¾ by 1¼ inches. Tape to your doll's hand.

Dollhouse furniture is generally made on a scale of 1 inch to a foot. A 6-foot sofa, for instance, would be made as a 6-inch replica for the average doll rooms and dollhouses. This is a rule of thumb for making miniature furniture. When you plan to copy a piece of real furniture, first measure the piece, then use this scale to adapt its measurements.

The materials most commonly used to make dollhouse furniture are heavy cardboard from packing cartons, posterboard of medium weight, parts of cigar boxes, and wood scraps ½ to ¼-inch thick. I cut cardboard and posterboard with a mat knife, but I generally carve wood with a very sharp kitchen knife that is easy for me to handle. You can finish wood with regular stain or paint, but use paint on cardboard or posterboard. Use epoxy glue to join parts, and white glue to attach fabric coverings.

Figure B shows the essential parts required to make furnishings similar to some of those in the dollhouses on pages 594 and 595. Major techniques used in making upholstered furniture are shown in photographs 3 to 6, which explain how the wing chair pattern is translated into a dollhouse toy. When I am working on a piece such as this, I make a paper pattern from which to cut the frame parts and the fabric. For simpler pieces, I draw the parts directly on the wood or cardboard.

A pocket mirror framed with a gold-lace-paper doily makes a dining-room mirror. An Oriental greeting card, set upright, becomes a room divider. A coaster glued to a piece of cardboard tubing serves as a coffee table. Books can be made from inch-square leaves cut from old magazines. Improvising accessories for the rooms is what makes furnishing a dollhouse such fun.

A wing chair is one of the easiest and most satisfactory pieces of furniture to make. It looks professionally made, and is sturdy enough to withstand many hours (and even years) of play. Use lightweight cardboard for the frame, (wings, back, seat) and, for upholstery, cotton fabric with a small design.

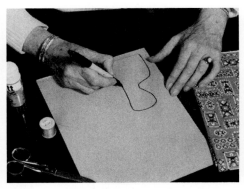

3: Trace wing chair patterns from figure B for two wings, a back, and a seat on cardboard as the first step. Then cut fabric to match the traced patterns.

4: Glue fabric to outside of each wing, overlapping to inside. Glue back fabric at top and down rear, and seat back at front only. Leave arm, unglued.

5: Stuff open sections of wing, arm and seat with cotton. Pack seat and top of wing tightly; use less stuffing for arm. Finish gluing fabric.

6: Sew wings to back after stuffing back. Wing fabric was cut with wrong side of fabric together, so pattern would be reversed. Fit finished seat between arms.

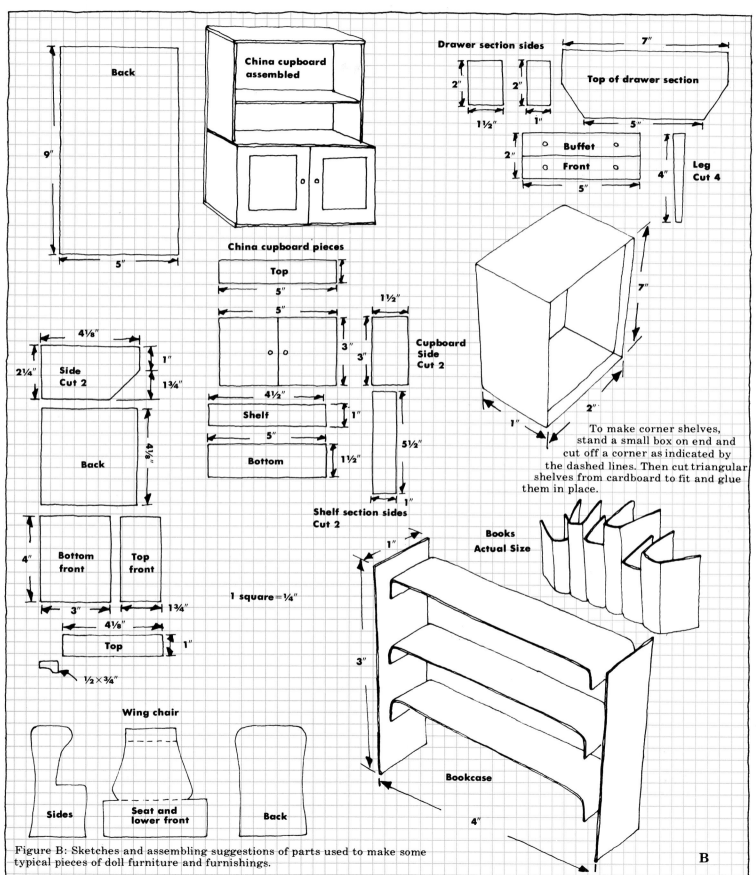

Back

9"

5"

China cupboard assembled

Drawer section sides

2" 2"

1½" 1"

7"

Top of drawer section

5"

2" **Buffet**

Front

5"

4" **Leg Cut 4**

4⅛"

2¼" **Side Cut 2** 1" 1¾"

Back

4⅛"

China cupboard pieces

Top

5"

5"

3" 3"

1½"

Cupboard Side Cut 2

Shelf

4½" 1"

5"

Bottom

1½"

5½"

1"

Shelf section sides Cut 2

7"

2"

1"

To make corner shelves, stand a small box on end and cut off a corner as indicated by the dashed lines. Then cut triangular shelves from cardboard to fit and glue them in place.

Bottom front **Top front**

4"

3" 1¾"

4⅛"

Top

1"

½ × ¾"

1 square = ¼"

1"

3"

Books Actual Size

Bookcase

4"

Wing chair

Sides **Seat and lower front** **Back**

Figure B: Sketches and assembling suggestions of parts used to make some typical pieces of doll furniture and furnishings.

B 597

Dollhouse people (unlike the larger dolls shown in "Dolls and Doll Clothing," page 604), must be small enough to fit into their houses. But they can still be made to sit, stand, and bend in various postures. Make bodies from patterns in figure C, tracing as in photograph 7. Wire legs and arms and assemble figure as in photographs 8 to 10. Using the patterns for clothing in figure C, dress this basic mannequin to suit your dollhouse room. Add elegant little scraps of satin and silk and fur for special-occasion costumes. The entry "Costumes", beginning page 526, suggests costumes for several periods. Embroider or, with a felt pen, draw shoes; or glue pieces of shiny black vinyl to the feet.

The elegant lady in black velvet has tiny pearls sewn at her neckline, matched by pearls glued on her shoes. The shoes were drawn on with a black felt pen. Her taffeta petticoat is ruffled.

7: Trace body pattern on double thickness of unbleached muslin. Stitch along outline before cutting. Leave top of head and two inches under the arm open.

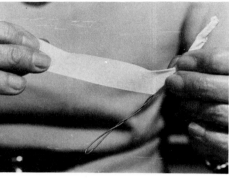

8: Double a 10-inch piece of 14-gauge wire, and twist it to form legs. Wrap wire with inch-wide strips of muslin, so wire won't puncture cloth of body.

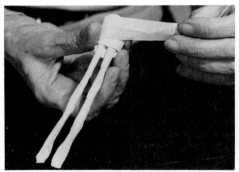

9: Tie wrapped legs together at top with muslin strips. Insert wire legs through side opening. Use pencil to stuff cotton into legs and body.

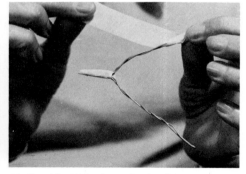

10: Double 12 inches of wire for arms; twisted ends form neck. Wrap wire with muslin, and insert in body. Stuff arms, head with cotton. Sew up openings.

When you make clothes for these miniature dollhouse people, it is wise to sew them onto the dolls. If the ladies wear short skirts, as does the maid in the dining room on page 595, cut narrow strips of nylon stockings, and sew or glue them (with white glue) to the legs. To dress a man in white tie and tails, use selvages of fabric scraps for the upstanding white collar, and glue or sew the coat front to the body, from the neck to the waist.

Faces for these tiny folk can be embroidered or drawn with a fine pen. Often a combination is used—for instance, eyebrows embroidered and eyes drawn. Give cheeks—both men's and women's—a touch of red crayon or rouge. And when men dolls have short haircuts, don't forget to provide ears, drawn or embroidered. To make hairdos for ladies, see photographs 11 to 14.

11: For a long hairdo, sew embroidery cotton in 4-inch lengths on doll's head. The stitching runs from front to back of head and forms the doll's part.

12: For a pigtail hairdo, use 8-inch strands of embroidery cotton, and stitch from side to side across head. Braid pigtails; tie with bows; cut bangs.

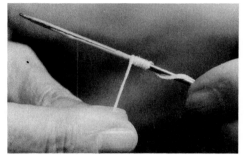

13: To form tight curls, wrap embroidery cotton around a steel knitting needle; run a thread of glue along cotton. When glue is dry, slip curl off the needle.

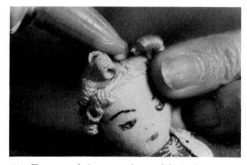

14: For an elaborate, formal hairdo, attach several tight curls to doll's head. Glue them to hair already sewed or glued to the head.

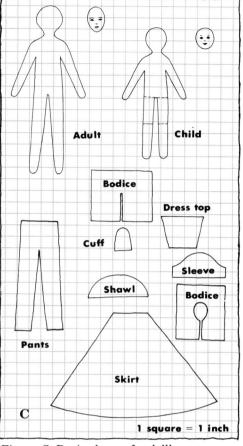

Figure C: Basic shapes for dollhouse people and their clothes.

This doll's formal gown and open mouth show that she was designed as a singer. The petticoat keeps her skirt in place.

Father, dressed in a dark-blue suit and dotted tie, relaxes on a cut-velvet sofa. His shoes are made of vinyl scraps.

599

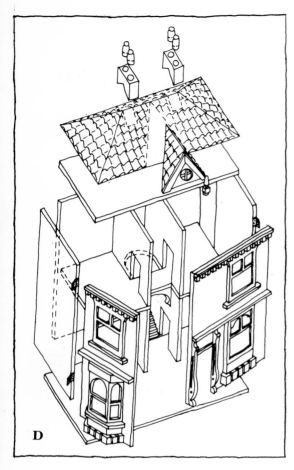

Figure D: This is how the major structural parts of the dollhouse fit together. Two front sections hinged to side walls open wide as in the photograph opposite. Tile roofing on the original model was painted on, but corrugated cardboard simulates tile more realistically if it is stripped on one side, cut, overlapped and painted.

The nineteenth-century dollhouse shown opposite and on page 592 is a two-story structure with a hip roof, window arches on the first floor, and an oculus (round) window in the top gable. Its overall dimensions are about 18 by 35 by 37 inches. Each room has a fireplace. A split staircase with a landing goes from the center hall on the first floor to the second floor. The front wall is made in two pieces, each hinged to a side wall. This is so that the front can be opened, as you can see in the photograph opposite. This, of course, makes for easy entry.

Although the house appears to be elaborately detailed, making one like it is not difficult. The plans given here do not provide an exact replica of the original. Some details have been simplified to make construction easier. Acetate windows are used in place of glass. All joints are butt-joined and fastened with white glue and finishing nails. To build the house you will need a hammer, nail set, crosscut handsaw, keyhole or saber saw, block plane, rasp, sanding block, drill with a 1-inch bit, penknife, adjustable square, ruler, pencil, screwdriver, paintbrushes, and scissors. The materials you will need are listed with the drawings on the opposite page.

Figure D shows how the major structural parts of the house are assembled. These parts are cut from 4-by-8 and 4-by-4 panels of ½-inch plywood, following the pattern layouts in figure E. Figure F gives detailed dimensions for each part and for the cutouts to be made in some of them. The dotted lines indicate where the walls and floor are joined. To determine the sloping sides of the triangular roof ends and dormer front, run a perpendicular line from the center point on the base of the triangle to the vertical distance indicated; mark this point, and then draw the triangle's sides from this point to the edges of the base. Use the same technique for the main roof sections, figure F, but measure 6½ inches from each side of the perpendicular to establish the points from which lines are drawn to the edges of the base. Dormer roof sections are right-angle triangles. You measure the distance shown on each leg from the right angle; then you simply draw the diagonal line.

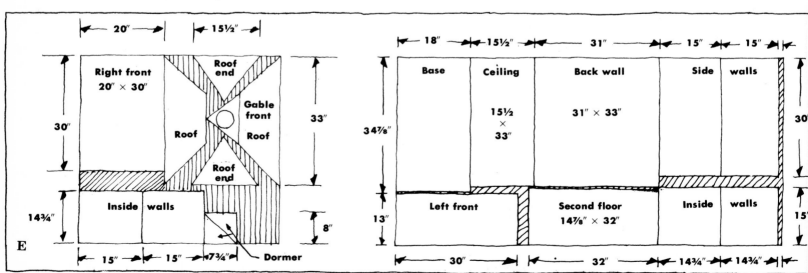

Figure E: Structural parts are cut from 4-by-4 and 4-by-8 foot panels of ½-inch plywood. Lay the parts out on the panels as shown.

Materials Needed for Wooden Doll House
4 by 8 foot panel of ½-inch plywood
4 by 4 foot panel of ½-inch plywood
3 feet of ¼ by 1¼-inch wood strips
3 feet of 1¼ by 1¼-inch wood strips
1 foot of 1 by 1-inch wood strips
1 by 2 by 7-inch pine board
½ by ¾ by 33-inch pine board
2 pieces, ½ by 2 by 14-inch board
(entry trim)
2 pine boards, 2½ by 4 by 4½-inches
15 inches of 1-inch diameter dowel
6 square feet of corrugated cardboard
Sheet of ⅛-inch acrylic (for windows)
4 lightweight butterfly hinges, 3-inch
Sandpaper in No. 60, 80, 100, 120 grades
Finishing nails in 1 and 1½-inch
lengths, 1 pound of each
Red, gray, glossy white, orange or buff,
and green paints, 1 pint each
Brown paper (to be ruled for floors),
Small-patterned contact paper or wallpaper for
walls, wool or double-knit scraps for
carpeting, rugs; small pictures (with
tape frames) cut from magazines.

15: With front panels open, you can see the fireplace units centered in each room, and the split stairway with landing midway between the first and second floors. For a view of this nineteenth-century dollhouse with the front sections closed, see page 592.

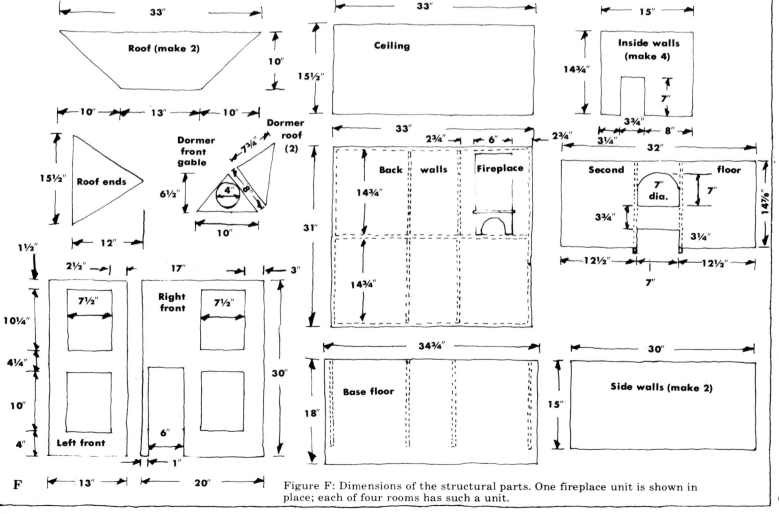

Figure F: Dimensions of the structural parts. One fireplace unit is shown in place; each of four rooms has such a unit.

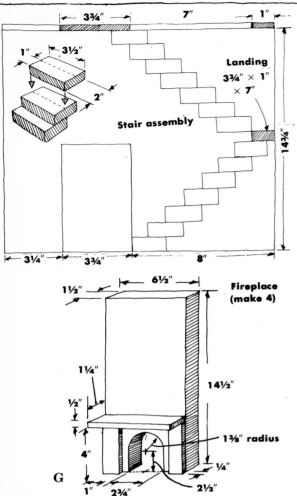

Figure G: Stairway and fireplace details.

After sawing and shaping the main structural pieces from plywood, cut out the details of the fireplace, stairs, dormer, chimney parts, windows, and window and door trim. Follow the dimensions given in figures G, H, I and J, and use pine boards, wood strips, or doweling as indicated. Follow the patterns given, but don't be afraid to draw some details freehand, such as the hallway arch, and the tops of the side arches of the bay window. Even the original dollhouse was not precisely dimensioned. Unless you have a lathe and know how to use it, use a pocket knife to whittle the tops of the chimney pots and the spire that fits on the dormer.

To make the bay window, with its seemingly complex angles, use one of the forms shown in figure H as a template, or pattern; overlap the appropriate window frame, sill, top, or base parts, and score the overlaps to mark the bevels needed. If you want to simulate glass in the windows, cut from a ⅛-inch acetate sheet the pieces to fit each window, and glue to window frames before attaching windows to house.

After all pieces have been cut out, sanded, and tested for fit, it is a good idea to paint and decorate the interior before assembling the house. The color photograph on page 601 shows some decorative ideas, but you can design your own. Paint the interior walls or glue small-patterned wallpaper or oil cloth on them. Cover floors with brown paper, lined to represent boards, or with wool or double-knit fabric for carpeting. Assemble stairs and landing as in figure G, and paint or stain them.

First step in assembly is to glue the first flight of stairs, with landing attached, to the first-floor inside wall on the right of the center hallway (see photograph 15 and figure G). Then glue the second flight to the opposite inside wall. Next, nail the first-floor inside walls to the base; the dotted lines in figure F on page 601 show where these interior walls fit on the base. Glue hallway arch in place between interior walls. Nail second floor to second-floor interior walls. Then glue this second-floor assembly on top of the first-floor interior walls; drive a few nails at an angle into the first-floor walls to hold the parts until the glue sets. Next, place assembly face down, and nail side walls to the second floor and to the base, spacing them in from the sides of the base as shown in figure F, and nailing through the base into the side walls.

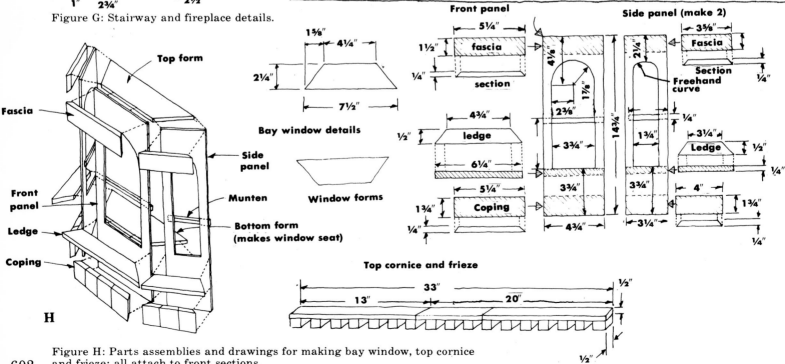

Figure H: Parts assemblies and drawings for making bay window, top cornice and frieze; all attach to front sections.

Assemble each fireplace unit, figure G, and glue the units to the back wall, figure F, centering one in each of the four rooms. At this time, you may decorate the fireplace units and the rear wall areas to match the other walls of the rooms. Then fasten the back wall, with fireplace units attached, to the side walls with nails (or No. 4, 1-inch screws if you expect to remove this wall frequently). Now nail the second-floor ceiling to the side and interior walls. Test fit the larger front and back roof sections to the ceiling, matching their corners to the ceiling corners. You will have to bevel the inside edges of each roof piece with a plane or a rasp to get a flat fit against the ceiling and between the joining parts of the roof pieces. Fit the roof ends onto the ceiling and between the roof sides the same way, beveling edges as necessary.

When you are satisfied with the fit, glue all the main roof pieces to the ceiling and to each other where they join. (A precise fit is not critical, because these parts will be covered with roofing.)

Glue the dormer front, framing, spire, and crossed window muntins together, figure J, and then attach the dormer to its roof sections and the roof as you did the other roof pieces, beveling the edges that meet and then gluing. Assemble the chimneys and their pots, figure I, and glue to the roof as in figure D. Glue window parts and trim, doorway trim, cornice boards and frieze at the top of the house to the two front sections that open, as shown in figures D, H, and J. Then fit front sections to the sides of the house. Fit four hinges to front pieces and sides, figure D, but do not attach permanently until after you have painted and decorated.

All trim is painted gloss-white; and outside walls are red, lined with gray if you wish to simulate brick. The roof of the original house is painted-on green roofing tile, but you can make more realistic tiles by separating plies of corrugated cardboard. Cut it into ½-inch-wide strips, and glue the strips to the roof, over-lapping them like real tiles, as in figures D and I. Paint tiles green. Chimneys are brick-red. Chimney pots are orange or buff. Paint black spots on top of pots for holes. Around the base of the bay window and box window score the wood with a pocket knife to represent separations between stones, and paint stones light gray.

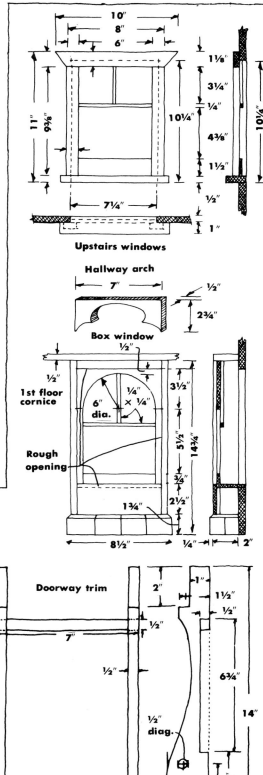

Upstairs windows

Hallway arch

Box window

1st floor cornice

Rough opening

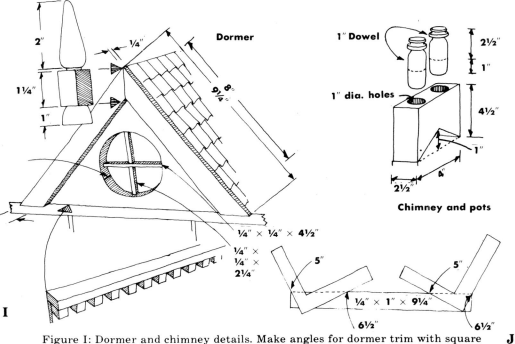

I

Figure I: Dormer and chimney details. Make angles for dormer trim with square as at lower right.

Figure J: Window and doorway trim details. 603

DOLLS AND DOLL CLOTHES
People For a Small World

There is something of magic in the making of a doll. With a few scraps of cloth, a piece of cardboard, and some glue, you can fashion a figure that acquires a personality of its own as you add a face and a hairdo. By the time you have put in the last stitches, given the doll a name, and placed it in the arms of a waiting child, the doll is ready to become a very real part of your household.

During the early years of U.S. history, when elaborate dolls were hard to come by, pioneer mothers made do with what was at hand, as the Indians had long been doing. They fashioned dolls from the husks of corn (page 610), and they used the shells of eggs (page 607) and nuts and fruits (pages 606 and 609) for heads. In the late 1800s, they used clothespins to make the kinds of dolls shown on page 608. Patterns for clothes for the dolls with walnut, egg, and dried-apple heads are on page 607. Many dolls like those from early days are still being made in the mountains of the eastern United States, where the old crafts continue to be practiced in traditional ways.

In the nineteenth century, cloth dolls, like Pauline Fischer's on page 612, and my great-grandmother's, below, became available, particularly in urban areas. Today, many of them are in antique-doll collections. These dolls were expensive even in their day, and techniques for repairing them developed. Some of these techniques are given in the Craftnotes, on page 611.

Margaret Perry, the author of this entry, also wrote "Dollhouses and Furniture" (pages 592–603) in this volume.

▲ This 1830 doll belonged to Peg Perry's great-grandmother, who learned to sew by making the doll wardrobe that is kept in the miniature trunk.

◄ Dollmaking techniques from Colonial days produced this collection of 3- to 6-inch charmers. Instructions for making each doll—with a dried apple, walnut, cloth pieces, cornhusk, or eggs—are given on the following pages.

Toys and Games
Walnut and egg dolls

The materials you will need for one walnut-head doll are: an English walnut (any size); a 14-inch square of light cardboard; a pipe cleaner, 7 inches long; a yard of white yarn; strips of cotton batting; masking tape; a felt pen; white glue; ⅛ yard of calico for dress and bonnet.

For the hairdo, glue the yarn to one side of the nut in a continuing spiral (photograph 1); start where the halves of the shell come together. Cover the back of the head with this spiraled yarn.

The shell joint makes a perfect nose for the doll. With a fine-pointed black felt pen (photograph 2), draw four curved lines for eyebrows and eyelids; make two large dots for eyes, two tiny dots (one on each side of the joint) for the nose, and a tiny slightly upcurving line for the mouth.

The doll's body is a cardboard cone 6 inches high. On the square of flexible cardboard, draw a circle 12 inches in diameter. From this, cut out a quarter section, and bend it into a cone. Fasten edges together with masking tape. Cut half an inch off the point, so the walnut will sit easily on top of the cone. Glue the walnut head to the cone.

Cut or punch a small hole in each side of the cone near the top; put the pipe cleaner through the holes, to make arms; secure with tape (photograph 3). Wrap cotton around arms for thickness and to hold clothing (photograph 4).

Following the patterns on the opposite page, cut out skirt, bodice, sleeves, and bonnet. Sew seams, and sew sleeves to bodice. Gather skirt at waist. The dress can be sewed or glued on; the bonnet is glued to the head.

The bodies and clothes for the egg-head dolls pictured on the opposite page are made the same way.

1: Glue white yarn for hair to walnut in a continuous spiral. Use a toothpick to spread white glue across the shell joint. Hold yarn in place until glue dries.

2: Draw facial features with a fine-pointed black felt pen. The features should be small and delicate. Practice drawing them on spare walnuts.

3: Secure pipe-cleaner arms to cone with masking tape. Crisscross the tape over the shoulder area. This will give additional shape to the top of the cone.

4: Wrap arms with cotton batting. Tie it firmly at the wrists to prevent slipping. Dress sleeves will fit over the cotton. The arms can be bent to any position.

Three walnut-head gossips stand chatting on a shelf in an antique corner cupboard. Natural variations in the walnut shells and in the hand-drawn features give each doll a unique character, although all were made the same way.

5: With the fine point of small, sharp scissors, make a tiny hole in each end of the eggshell. Then blow into one hole. This will expel the contents.

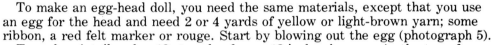

Eggshells are an especially good shape to form the heads of dolls dressed in calico and gingham. The hair of the doll wearing the bonnet is done in a bun.

To make an egg-head doll, you need the same materials, except that you use an egg for the head and need 2 or 4 yards of yellow or light-brown yarn; some ribbon, a red felt marker or rouge. Start by blowing out the egg (photograph 5).

To make pigtails, glue 12 strands of yarn 12 inches long across the top of the head, starting just at the forehead and continuing down the back. Make two braids (photograph 6), and tie on ribbons matching the dress fabric. To make a bun, use 6-inch strands of yarn; glue on the same way, but fold up the ends and tie them into a bun with thread.

Draw the doll's face with a fine-pointed black felt pen. Put a touch of color on the lips and cheeks with a red felt marker or rouge.

6: When the yarn has been glued to the head, divide it into two sets of six strands, and braid the pigtails. Tie on ribbon bows, and trim pigtail ends.

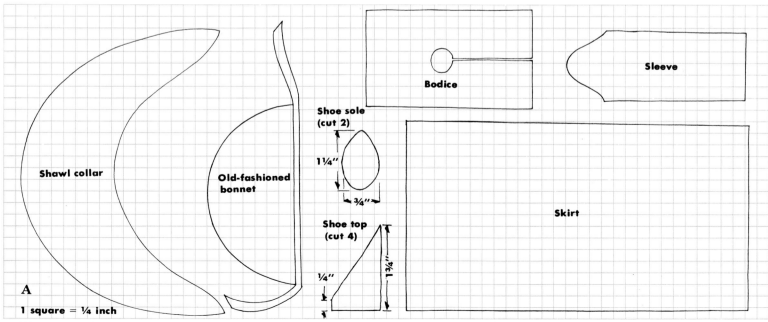

Figure A: Patterns for costumes for walnut-head, egg-head, and dried-apple-head dolls.

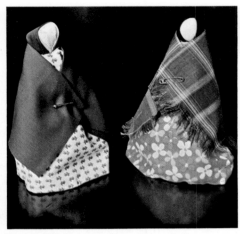

The traditional Indian pieces doll, a favorite with the Sioux Indians of South Dakota, does not have a face. Scraps of any size can be used to make these dolls. They stand, held up by the bunching of the fabric they are made of.

Toys and Games
Pieces doll

This traditional Indian doll is made entirely of scraps of material—hence its name. The size depends on the size of the scraps. To make one like those pictured at left, you will need pieces of white and colored material, white glue, a safety pin, and string or strong thread.

First, roll a 6-inch square of white cloth into a ball, to make the head. Drape a 6-inch square of white cloth over this, for the body; tie it around the neck with thread. Next, drape a folded piece of dark cloth (slightly smaller than the white) over the head; tie it at the neck as well.

The dress can be crudely cut from a 3-by-6-inch piece of fabric folded into a square. Cut each side up at a slight angle toward the fold; then out to the edge, to make sleeves. Sew the side seams. Cut a hole in the fold for the doll's head. The cloak is a 5-inch square of fabric, folded to make a rectangle and fastened horizontally with a safety pin. No edges are finished except the dress hem, and this can be sewed or glued.

Making pieces dolls is a popular activity for children's parties.

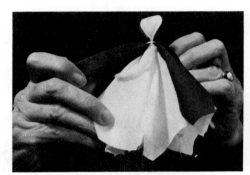

7: For the head covering of the pieces doll, here seen from the front, fold a square of dark fabric, and tie it around the neck. Material helps form the body.

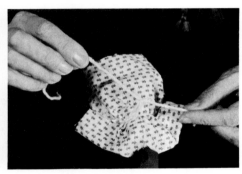

8: Tie the simple dress at the waist. Side seams are sewed, but the hem of the dress shown here is glued. This back view shows the doll's dark head covering.

Miniature home-made dolls, such as this clothespin doll held by five-year-old Ursina Amsler, have tremendous appeal for your children.

Toys and Games
Clothespin doll

The materials needed to make a clothespin doll are: a wooden clothespin; a handful of polyester fiber filling or absorbent cotton; three ¼-by-4-inch strips of nylon; a ½-inch-wide strip of lacy nylon; a pipe cleaner, 4 inches long; a 3-by-8-inch piece of calico; a 3-by-8-inch piece of crinoline; string.

Pad the rounded top of the clothespin with ⅛-inch-thick polyester fiber or cotton. Cover the padded head with a nylon strip (cut from a slip or light-color hose), and tie the strip around the neck with string. Next, pad the chest area with polyester ¼-inch thick. Cover this padding with another nylon strip, and tie the strip around the waist. For the arms, wrap a pipe cleaner with a third nylon strip, and sew it horizontally to the center of the doll's back. Crisscross the chest area with a strip of lacy nylon, to form the blouse. Sew the blouse pieces securely at the waist.

The full skirt is stiffened with an underskirt of crinoline. Gather both the calico and the crinoline at the waist (the 8-inch sides), and sew tightly to the doll. Trim the crinoline and hem the skirt so that they just cover the bottom of the clothespin. The fabric holds the doll upright. Glue yarn to the head to make an attractive hairpiece, and use a felt-tip pen to color the lips and eyes.

Toys and Games
Apple-head doll

To make an apple-head doll, you will need: a firm apple; two cloves; four tiny pebbles; yarn; ¼ yard of calico; black felt and silk scraps for shoes; hat and reticule; strips of cotton sheet; 6 feet of 14-gauge wire; cotton; white glue; rouge; clear lacquer; white thread; a tiny feather. Pare the apple; remove a small wedge on each side of the nose. Cut out ¼-inch holes for eye sockets. Make a curved slit, ¾-inch long, for the mouth. Push a clove into each eye socket. (photograph 9). Embed the pebbles in the mouth slit for teeth. Shape a 12-inch piece of 14-gauge wire and insert it through the head, (photograph 10), leave a loop at the top and hang the apple from it to dry. The ends of the wire, extending from the neck, will later be used to attach head to body. Mold the apple features daily while it dries. In about a week, lacquer the apple and rouge lips and cheek. Make a T-shape armature (photograph 11) from about 5 feet of wire, with arms 5, neck 1, legs 8 inches long. The wire goes down and up one leg, then the other, out to form an arm, across to the other arm and back. Twist where wires meet, to firm the body. Wrap with strips of sheet tied with thread. Twist together body and head wires. Glue on enough yarn hair to show under the hat. Patterns for costume and black felt shoes are on page 607. Glue the two triangular top sections at the instep and center of the heel. Glue on the oval sole. Make the hat from a 2-by-4-inch piece of felt; draw a 3-inch-diameter circle (brim) and, inside it, a 1½-inch-diameter circle (crown top). Cut out. Glue both to a ½-inch-wide felt band. Glue on the feather. Make reticule from a 4-inch-diameter circle of silk. Stitch around the edge, fill with ball cotton, draw the thread, and as the final step, tie it to the doll's hand.

This dried-apple-head doll was made by Margaret Tallardy of Southington, Conn., whose dolls are featured at many New England craft festivals and fairs.

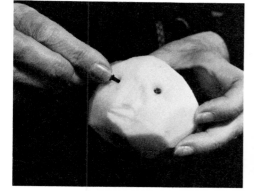

9: Place cloves in eye sockets after features have been carved in pared apple. When the apple is dry, put a dot of white paint in the center of each clove, or replace the cloves with buttons.

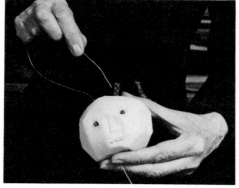

10: Push wire bent to U-shape through the core of the apple, from the top of the head to the neck. Leave a loop at the top for hanging the apple while it dries. Twist wire ends together at the neck.

11: Pad the T-shape wire armature at the arms and chest to give the body form. Sew the clothes to this padded frame. Neck wire of armature is twisted with wires from the apple to join head to body.

Toys and Games
Cornhusk doll

It is generally believed that the Indians taught early American settlers to make dolls of cornhusks, the outer covering on an ear of corn. Today, this is a popular craft project (see the light-green cornhusk doll on page 604). You can dye cornhusks any color, as shown at left.

You will need husks from six ears of corn; dye or vegetable coloring; string; a 7-inch pipe cleaner; a black felt pen. Soak the husks in lukewarm water five minutes; leave them in the water while you make the doll. To make the head, tear off a ¼-inch-wide strip the full length of a husk, and roll it into a ball (photograph 12). Add more strips until the ball is ¾ inch in diameter. Pin, or tie in place with string. For the upper body, make a ball 1½ inches in diameter. To make arms, wind inch-wide strips around pipe cleaner (photograph 13); tie at the wrists with string or very narrow strips of husk.

To assemble head, arms, and upper body, start by draping a long, inch-wide piece of husk over the head (photograph 14). The inside of the husk should be on the outside; it makes a smoother face. Twist the ends to form a neck, and tie. Place the arms just under the neck, the upper body under the arms, and tie the husk below the upper body with string (photograph 15).

To make the skirt, place a layer of full-length husks, pointed ends up, around the waistline; tie securely. Add and tie husk layers until the skirt is very full, for this is what the doll stands on. Cut off husks evenly at the bottom. Add a bouffant overskirt if you like (photograph 16).

Make a bodice of two husk strips, ½ inch wide, crossed front and back and tied at the waist (photograph 17). Then cover the waistline with a ½-inch-wide husk sash, tied securely.

For hair, glue corn silk to the head. To make a bonnet, tie a 1-by-5-inch husk strip around head, and cut off excess. After doll has dried, draw facial features with a fine-pointed black felt pen. Sometimes only eyes and two tiny dots for the nose are drawn. If you draw a mouth, make it small.

Use your imagination to devise an umbrella from a pipe cleaner, or make a broom of twigs, for the cornhusk doll to carry.

Colored cornhusks show a few of the hues that can be achieved by dyeing. Use fabric dye that dissolves in cold water, and leave the husks in the bath for only a few minutes for a light tone, longer for a deeper shade. If you have vegetable coloring, you can use that to color cornhusks. You can work with the wet husks immediately after they have soaked in the coloring or dye. If they have dried out, soak them again in lukewarm water so you can shape them. Wet husks may be turned inside-out.

12: Roll cornhusk strips into balls to form the head and body. Secure each ball with a short straight pin or tie with string.

13: Wind inch-wide strips of husk around a pipe cleaner to form the arms. Arms can be bent even after husk dries.

14: Drape a strip of husk over head, long enough to cover arms and upper body. Secure it under the head with string.

15: Slip arms and an upper-body ball under the husk strip covering the head. Tie strip under the body ball, at waist.

16: To make a bouffant overskirt, tie husks at the waist, as shown; then let ends fall down over the string.

17: Add bodice husk strips and hide ends and skirt top with a 1/2-inch-wide sash. For security, use string to tie in waist.

DOLL CRAFTNOTES

In the nineteenth century, lifelike dolls with china or papier-mache heads were produced commercially. They were expensive toys. Unlike the expendable early Colonial dolls, they were too precious to discard when parts were damaged, and putting them back together again became an art.

The techniques developed then are used today, only a little updated. Some repairs—eye malfunctions, for instance—are best made at a doll hospital. Replacement parts can be purchased from many doll hospitals, collectors, and from mail order houses such as Yield House, North Conway, N.H., 04860; Mark Farmer Company, Inc., 36 Washington Avenue, Point Richmond, Calif. 94801; Jennifer House, Great Barrington, Mass. 01320; Old Guilford Forge, Guilford, Conn. 06437; Irma's Dolls, Route No. 2, Rome, Ohio 44805; Sullivan's, New Market, Md., 21774.

You can make new parts for a cloth body by adapting the principles used in the pattern, figure C, for Pauline Fischer's doll on pages 612 and 613. Or take the doll apart; make patterns from the parts; cut and sew them. Today, polyester fiber from the five-and-dime store is generally used as filling for cloth dolls.

Other problems easily repaired at home are these:

Lost eyelashes: Replace eyelashes with individual artificial lashes cut from those sold in strips at the beauty counters of drug stores. Lay the doll down, so its eyes close. With a toothpick, put a thread of white glue on one eyelid. With tweezers, place a single lash, and hold it until dry. Continue until lost lashes have been restored.

Cracks in finish: With a toothpick, smear the whole cracked area with a thin, smooth film of ceramic cement, sold at art-supply shops. As the cement begins to dry, press the edges of the crack firmly together, and hold until glue dries. It will dry clear, filling in the cracks.

Hair repair: Wigs suitable for dolls are sold in various sizes by doll hospitals in large cities. Before attaching a new wig, scrape off old glue, and wash the head with a cloth dampened in warm water. Wipe the head dry, and paint it with a thin coat of white glue. Position the wig, and hold it until the glue begins to set. After 24 hours, trim the wig to the desired length.

Limb joints: Jointed dolls that have become unstrung are easy to put together again, as shown in Figure B. To string a 12-inch doll, you will need one 12-inch and one 8-inch length of elastic. At each of the joints, there should be hooks for the elastic. If any of these hooks have been lost, fashion new ones from a 10-gauge wire; set into original holes; fill and seal in with ceramic cement.

Fasten the elastic to the hooks at the points shown in figure B. Center the elastic through the neck hook. Thread the ends through the body, out the leg openings, and pull the elastic to draw the head to the body. On the left side of the body, loop the elastic through the hook attached to the left leg. Then thread the left end back through the opening, across the body, and out through the right-leg opening. Loop the right end of the elastic through the right-leg hook. Knot the ends, making the knot larger than the eye of the hook.

To connect the doll's arms, center the 8-inch piece of elastic through the right-arm hook and pull both ends of the elastic through the body and out the left-arm hole. Pass one end through the left-arm hook and tie the ends together.

Irving Chais, owner of the New York Doll Hospital, in New York City, carries on the business his father founded in the early 1900s.

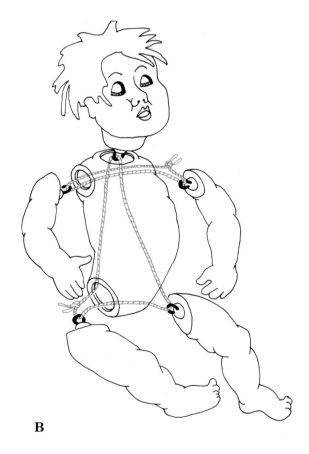

B

Figure B: To tie elastic, make a single overhand knot and pull the ends almost taut. Maintain this tension while you make a square knot. The elastic should pull arms, legs and head into place. Test joints by placing doll in sitting and standing positions. Then trim ends of elastic and tuck them inside the body.

Toys and Games
Cloth doll

This old-fashioned cloth doll made by Pauline Fischer 25 years ago for her daughter appears in the hand-applique section of the entry "Applique" in Volume One. The original doll's body is made of white muslin; face, arms and neck of pink muslin; and the back of the head of yellow muslin matching the yarn hair. Instructions for the adaptation of the doll, given in figure C, call for one color of fabric, flesh-colored muslin.

Making this old-fashioned doll is a challenge because the pattern has so many parts. You will need: a few strands of cotton embroidery floss, blue for the irises of the eyes, light brown for the brows, nose, freckles, poppy red for the mouth; two rounds of black felt for eye pupils; two skeins of cotton or wool rug yarn (yellow) for the hair; a large bag of polyester fiber for the filling; flesh-colored muslin or cotton, 1½ yards (36-inch width) or 1¼ yards (45-inch width), for the covering. To give the doll a finished look, press each seam open as it is completed, then turn it right side out and press again.

From figure C, prepare a paper pattern, following instructions on page 57, Volume One. Transfer all notches and markings. Pattern pieces lettered (a) are duplicates; two pieces of that number are required. Note that pattern piece 4 requires four pieces. Using the pattern, cut out the fabric pieces.

Embroidering the Face: On the face (piece 1) use satin stitch to embroider brows, irises, mouth; use seed stitch to embroider freckles; use outline stitch to embroider nose. See instructions for making these stitches in "Crewel", pages 538 to 549. Sew down felt pupils cut to size you will achieve when you have enlarged pattern piece 1.

Making the Head: With right sides of fabric facing, and double notches matched, sew chin, 2, to face, 1. Cut back of head, 3, completely apart along dashed interior lines. With right sides facing, stitch these pieces together again, matching notches to give head contour. Match notches at forehead centers of 1 and 3, and sew pieces together with right sides facing. Stop stitching where chin begins. Turn right side out. Stuff head with polyester filling.

Making the Arms: With right sides facing, sew together two arm pieces numbered 4. Right side out, stitch finger lines. Do not sew arm sockets closed. On wrong side, pin 5 to 4, matching the notch on 5 to the shoulder-top seam on 4. Sew 4 and 5 together on the three curved sides only, leaving a 1-inch opening around the notch in 5. Turn right side out. With polyester filling, stuff the arm full. Turn unsewn socket seam edges in, and handsew arm closed. With right side facing, sew up long and short seams. Turn right side out. Fold arm tab, 6, along the solid line. Tuck tab seam allowance into 1-inch opening left in arm top and handstitch. Make the right arm in the same way from pieces 4a, 5a, 6a.

Making the Body: With the right sides facing, use a double row of stitching to sew together the shoulder sections of the body, front and back, 7 and 8. Sew side sections 9, 9a, to 7 and 8, matching notches. Do not sew bottom seams. Turn right side out. Pin bottom seams securely together.

With right sides facing, sew together the sides of neck front and back, 10 and 11. Turn right side out. Match notches on 10 and 11 to the notches in the neck fronts of 7 and 8. On the right side, pin neck onto body, easing fabric around curves. Sew together by hand. Stuff body.

Making Legs and Feet: With right sides facing, sew the leg front, 12, to the vamp, 13, matching double notches. Sew 13 to 14, the sole, matching single notches. Sew 15, leg back, to 12, leg front, easing the heel into the sole. Turn leg right side out, stuff, and sew up the seam at the top of the leg (photograph 18). Prepare the other leg and foot from 12a, 13a, 14a, 15a. Unpin body seat bottom, pin leg tabs into place between bottom seams and sew up with a double row of stitching.

Finishing the Doll: Ease head down over neck and adjust stuffing. Handstitch into place around back with seam allowance turned in. Sew arm tabs securely to body shoulder. stitching chin.

To make the doll's hair, cut 45 36-inch strands of wool, fold them in half to make double 18-inch strands. At the fold, handstitch each strand to the doll's head at the hairline, beginning and ending at points level with the lower rim of her eyes (photograph 19). Trim the ends.

For related projects see: "Animal Dolls", "Applique", "Crewel", "Dollhouses", "Puppets", "Rag Dolls".

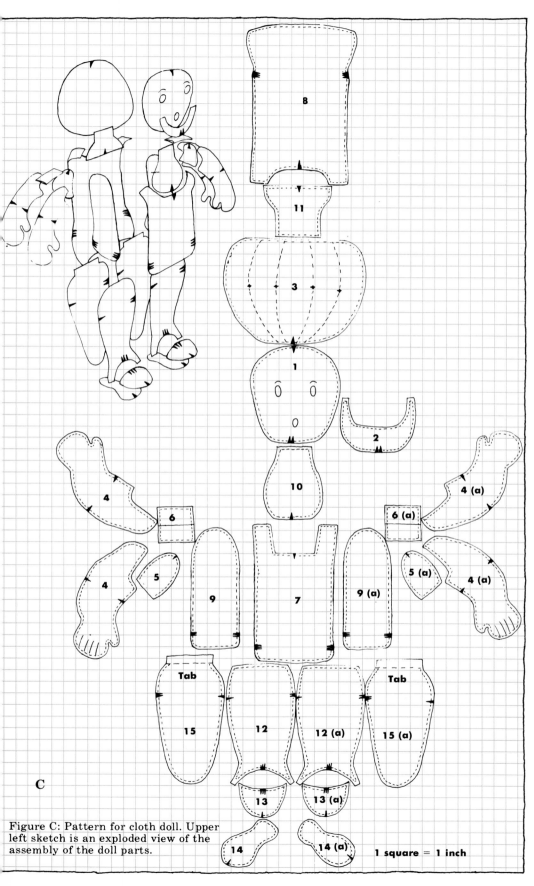

Figure C: Pattern for cloth doll. Upper left sketch is an exploded view of the assembly of the doll parts.

1 square = 1 inch

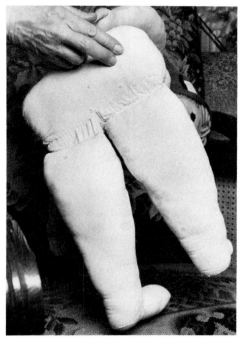

18: Tabs on the backs of the legs extend beyond the seam joining the front and back leg pieces, 12 and 15, at the top. Sew these seams on the right side of the fabric, after the leg has been assembled and stuffed. Then insert the tabs between the body front and back at the bottom, and handstitch into place.

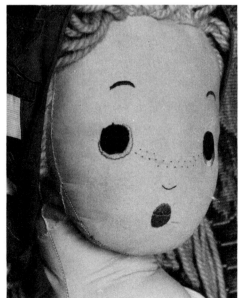

19: Close-up of the doll's face and neck shows use of satin stitch for the mouth and around the black felt pupils of the eyes, the seed stitch making the freckles, the outline stitch making the nose, and the way the finished head section fits down over the doll's neck. The wool strands making up the hair are sewed to the hairline, then pulled straight back from the doll's forehead.

DRIED FLOWERS
Beauty That Lasts

Georgia S. Vance—author of The Decorative Art of Dried Flower Arrangement, *published by Doubleday—has a consuming interest in flowers and gardens. An Army wife, she has traveled extensively and experimented with plants of all regions. She has been the first to dry many difficult flowers and is so expert in this craft that she teaches it to wives of diplomats for the U.S. State Department. Ms. Vance also prepares dried-flower arrangements for historic houses here and abroad.*

In a book entitled *Flora–Ouero Cultura di Fiori*, published in Rome in 1638, one P. Giovanni Battista Ferrari, of Siena, reserved a chapter for describing how "art and skill can keep alive and everlasting a thing as frail and deciduous as the flower." Ferrari gave practical how-to information about drying flowers in sand that is as relevant now as it was 300 years ago. With hardly a change of technique, Ferrari's method was described in an article published by Mathew Carey, of Philadelphia, in 1788.

We are still drying flowers in sand, though silica gel is a faster-drying agent, and the arrangement shown on page 618 is much like those you will find in historical restorations. Even the delightful little scented spice-and-seed bouquet on page 623 is a throwback to the fragrant tussie-mussies of Colonial times. If anything has changed, it probably is the variety of ingredients we now are willing to include in dried arrangements.

Found supplies are among my favorite sources for subjects for dried arrangements; it is lovely to preserve the fragile beauty of the flowers you grew during the summer, but the bouquets and arrangements take on other dimensions when they include mementoes of a walk along the shore or a ramble in the woods. Real oyster shells, gnarly roots, rose hips, anything you fancy that can be dried thoroughly—even oranges—can be used in your arrangements.

Drying with Sand

In one to three weeks, depending on flower thickness, sand will absorb all flower moisture, until only the dried tissues remain. Dried flowers are stiff, somewhat shrunken, but still colorful and beautiful in bouquets.

Sand is inexpensive and easy to get. It must be dry, clean, and fine-grained. Sand sold for sandboxes or concrete can be used without special preparation. Sea-beach or lake sand must be washed to remove salt, air- or oven-dried, and sifted to remove foreign material.

When sand is the drying agent, leave the container uncovered during the drying period. Bury flowers as explained on pages 616 and 617. Cardboard cartons, with seams taped shut, are ideal for sand-drying many flowers. Cookie tins and plastic storage boxes are good for smaller lots. Covered, they can be used also for silica-gel drying. Keep flowers being sand-dried in a warm, dry place (where humidity is 60 percent or less).

▲ Air-dried sunflower seed heads and wisteria branches make up a modern arrangement.

▶ Smaller and stiffer than when they were fresh, dried flower blossoms have immobility and fragility that give them a nostalgic beauty.

Flowers will not dry well in a cool, damp basement. In summer, the attic, where temperatures easily may reach 120F, is the best place for flower drying. Another good place is a gas oven with only the pilot light on; four days to a week of drying time there is enough for most flowers. You can remove the container when you want to bake.

Drying with Silica Gel

Silica gel should always be kept in a closed container when in storage and when drying flowers, with the exception noted below. Silica gel, a form of colloidal silica in fine granules for flower-drying use, is sold by most garden shops. It looks like white sand, but is lighter in weight. It is highly absorbent; unless covered, it will draw moisture from the air as well as from flowers. Blue crystals that turn white when saturated with moisture come mixed with the granules to indicate when the gel's drying capacity has ended. The gel can be reused many times before this happens. When it does happen, dry the gel in a 250F oven until the crystals turn blue again. After cooling, the gel will be as good as new.

Flowers dry faster in silica gel than in sand, but must be removed from the gel as soon as they are completely dried, or they may discolor and become brittle. There is no reliably definitive drying time for flowers in silica gel, as there are too many variables. The times the gel has been used affects drying time—the less saturated it is, the faster it will dry a flower. Flowers' moisture content affects drying time, and moisture depends on the season. Suggested drying times are given in the list below; they are approximate drying times. To guard against overdrying in gel, I place a test flower in a corner of the container, where I can check it often without disturbing the

Cockscomb contains little moisture and can be air-dried. See page 620.

other flowers. If you are drying many flowers in layers (thicker flowers on the bottom, thinner on top), put a test flower in each layer.

The oven method described for sand-drying also can be used with silica gel for quick drying. (Use only metal containers. Plastic would melt; cardboard might burn.) Leave the container uncovered, and place in a 150F to 180F oven. Allow 4 to 6 hours quick drying for each day of gel drying in list below.

Air-drying, preserving with glycerine, and pressing—additional methods of drying—are described on pages 620 and 621.

Suggested Drying Media and Times

This list includes flowers representative of all types of petal structure. Relate unlisted flowers to the closest structure type here to select a drying medium and to determine approximate drying time. Sand drying times, which are not critical, are discussed above.

Anemone—gel (3-4 days)
Carnation—gel (3 days)
Clematis—quick dry in gel (12-18 hrs.)
Daffodil—gel (3-4 days)
Delphinium—sand; gel (2-4 days)
Dogwood—sand is best
Feverfew—sand is best
Forget-me-not—sand; gel (2 days)
Globe thistle—air-dry (see page 620)
Hyacinth—sand; gel (5-6 days)
Hydrangea—sand; air-dry
Iris—gel (3-4 days)

Larkspur—sand is best
Lilac—sand; gel (2-3 days)
Lily—gel (4-5 days)
Lily-of-the-valley—sand; gel (2-3 days)
Magnolia—gel (4-5 days)
Marigold—sand; gel (3-4 days)
Pansy—quick dry in gel (12-18 hrs.)
Peony—sand; gel (5-6 days)
Poinsettia—sand; gel (4-5 days)
Rhododendron—gel (4-5 days)
Salvia—air-dry
Tulip—gel (4-5 days)

615

1: Materials needed include masking tape, pliers, clippers, drying container, sand or silica gel, florist's wire in 6-inch lengths, tin can for pouring, bowl to hold extra sand or silica gel.

2: Insert florist's wire into the flower's cut stem far enough to secure it in the flower base (calyx) but not so far that it will show after the flower has been shrunk by drying.

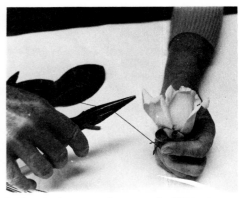

3: Bend wire at a sharp angle. With the flower set in the drying agent, the angled wire will stick up and make a handle that you can use to remove flower from container.

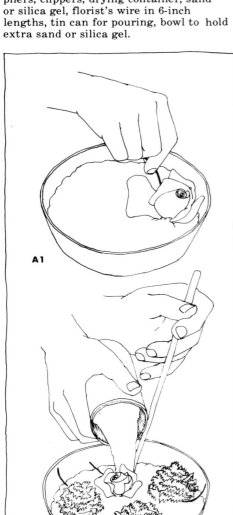

Figure A: Use angled wire as a handle to place flower (A1). Space flowers 1 inch from each other and container sides. Hold petals with a dowel as you pour (A2).

Preparations before Drying

To dry flowers that will remain natural-looking, you must prepare the fresh flowers very carefully. Whether these come from a florist or your garden, before they are dried it is important that they be crisp and fresh, their petal tissues filled with water. To freshen florist flowers, cut 1 or 2 inches from the stems, and stand them in water for a few hours or overnight. To keep garden flowers fresh, carry a water-filled container when you cut them, and place the cut flowers in it at once. To revive store-bought or picked flowers that have woody stems, make 2-inch-long slashes at the stem ends, and peel back the bark a little to provide more surface for water absorption.

Tools and Materials

These are the tools and materials I use for drying small batches of flowers: two- to three-quart plastic or tin container (with a cover if I am using silica gel), large enough to hold four or five flowers plus drying medium; at least two quarts of sand or silica gel; garden clippers; needle-nose mechanic's pliers with wire-cutting blades (handy for placing flowers in an arrangement as well as for cutting wire); 24-gauge florist's wire in 6-inch lengths; a bowl or container to hold the sand or gel for covering flowers; a tin can for scooping sand or gel; a chopstick or wooden dowel; masking tape to seal the drying container if I am using gel; white glue and a small camel's-hair watercolor brush to reattach any petals that may come loose during the drying; a roll of green florist's adhesive tape to attach stems to wire; some blocks of floral foam for arranging and storing.

Drying Flowers Face Up

Generally, only the head of a flower is dried; leaves are removed. The stems are wired or cut off and replaced by wire. To fill in for the missing leaves, air-dried filler materials, like those shown on the opposite page, are used.

Large-petal or dense flowers, such as dahlias and roses, are dried face up.

Pour enough sand or silica gel into the drying container to support flowers (1 to 2 inches). Cut off stems 1 inch below blossoms. From each stem, cut a straight, 2-inch length; set aside. These will be reattached later (see photograph 11, page 618) to give the flowers a natural appearance. Insert a 6-inch wire into the base of each flower (photograph 2), and bend as in photograph 3. Insert stem end and wire into drying medium so bottom petals are supported underneath and the wire protrudes from the medium (figure A1). Gently sift sand or gel over the flowers and into spaces between them, as shown in figure A2. Try to equalize the pressure of drying granules on all areas of the flowers so petal shape and position are not altered. If petals bend, hold them in place with fingers or a wooden dowel (figure A2).

Drying Flowers Face Down and Diagonally

Placing flowers in a face-down or a diagonal position for drying makes it possible to retain longer natural stems without increasing the depth of the drying medium. The diagonal position is well suited for multipetaled smaller flowers, such as marigolds, geum, cornflowers, small roses, and windflowers. The face-down position works best for single daisy-type flowers or any flowers with petals on a flat plane, such as Queen Anne's lace. Zinnias may be dried either diagonally or face down.

To provide for easy storage and arranging and to reinforce these longer stems, they are wired. Cut each stem to 3 to 5 inches in length, and insert a 6-inch length of florist's wire up through the stem to the base (calyx) of the flower. Flowers and stems shrink during drying, so don't push the wire too far into the flower or it may show. For wiring hollow-stem flowers, such as zinnias, see photograph 4.

For flowers to be dried diagonally, bend the wire at a right angle to the stem. Then make a small ridge across the drying medium (see photograph 5), and lean the flowers along the ridge, with the heads hanging free. Pour drying agent first behind and between the flowers (photograph 5) and then from side to side and in front. Continue until they are covered.

The wire for a flower to be dried face down is not angled (see photograph 5). Make an indentation in the drying medium that conforms to the shape of the flower face. If the flower is slightly cup shape, make a mound, and press the cup gently over it, so all surfaces touch the drying medium. Pour the medium over the flowers until they are just covered; too much medium above the flowers will cause shifting when the container is moved.

Store the flowers for drying as described on pages 614 and 615. Use the list on page 615 as a guide to drying times. Follow the instructions for photographs 9 to 13, page 618, for handling flowers when they are dry.

Dried bittersweet branches and berries, arranged here on driftwood, also make good filler material for other dried bouquets, filling in for missing leaves.

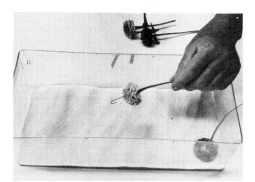

4: Wire for hollow-stem flowers, such as zinnias, is pushed all the way through stem and flower, bent into a hook, then pulled back until the hook is firmly embedded in the flower.

5: When pouring sand over flowers in a diagonal position (left), fill behind them first, then in front. When covering face-down flowers (right), pour from one to another, gradually increasing depth.

Nandina, porcelain-vine, bittersweet berries, and rose hips, make good fillers to use around the base of an arrangement.

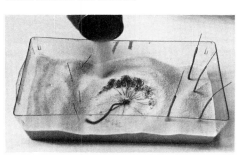

6: Queen Anne's lace, like other flowers with petals on a flat plane, is placed face down. When covering it, build up the sand around and inside the blossom simultaneously. The stem is not wired.

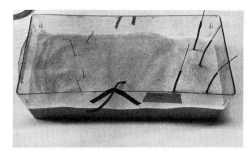

7: When flowers are covered, tape unwired stem to box. Label box with contents and date, and leave it uncovered, as sand is the medium. Such clear-plastic storage boxes are ideal for drying flowers.

Okra, goldenrod, and poppy seed pods that have been air-dried are other attractive fillers for bouquets.

617

8: Use a closed container for flowers drying in silica gel; seal the cover's edge with masking tape. Add a label that records the container's contents and the date when it was sealed.

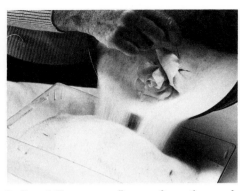

9: Carefully remove flowers from the sand or silica gel when the drying period is over. Tilt container so the medium pours out. As flowers become uncovered, grasp their wires, and gently pull them free.

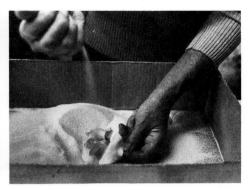

10: Run sand lightly over flowers dried in gel, to remove granules clinging to them. This is not necessary for flowers dried in sand. Keep this sandblasting sand separate from that used for drying.

Roses, lilacs, and air-dried cockscomb are among the elements of this bouquet. Large flower in the center is a peony.

11: Straighten the flower's wire, and push it through the stem section that was previously cut off and set aside (see text, page 616). If it is hard to get the wire through the preserved stem, use a length of fresh stem as a replacement.

12: Push the wire through the stem piece until flower's short stem rests on it. Wind wire with green florist's tape until it overlaps stem. Reattach any petals that drop off with water-diluted white glue applied with camel's-hair brush.

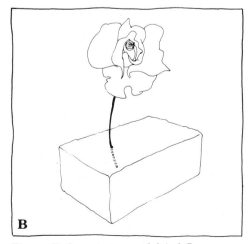

Figure B: Insert stems of dried flowers in blocks of floral foam for storage. This frees the flowers from any pressure that might damage the delicate petals.

13: Store dried flowers by inserting stems into floral foam (figure B) taped to the bottom of a cardboard box. Then seal the box in a plastic bag. This airtight container prevents humidity from seeping back into the flowers and helps screen out light, which might change flower colors.

Dried Mexican zinnias, black-eyed Susans, goldenrod, snowballs, and ferns make up a traditional arrangement. Zinnias on ledge are fresh. Can you tell the difference?

14: Containers for dried arrangements should have a generous base and a throat wide enough to contain a block of floral foam to hold the flower stems. Fill the base with sand. With a knife, shape the foam to fit snugly inside the container opening, rest on the sand, and extend an inch or so above the vase, as shown here. Secure the block to the container with strips of florist's tape.

Making Dried-Flower Arrangements

To make dried arrangements, you will need a container, sand to weight it, floral foam and florist's tape, and a selection of dried flowers and foliage (for how to preserve and press foliage, see page 620) or fillers. The pliers in photograph 1, page 616, are handy for placing flowers.

Like fresh flowers, dried ones should be arranged with careful attention to color and form. Because the arrangement will be around for a long time, take the trouble to find a container color and shape that will complement your arrangement. For the arrangement, choose a dominant color, then other colors that will blend or contrast with it. Add wire extensions to stems whenever necessary to improve flowers' position. I find dried flowers with wire stems easier to handle and arrange than fresh ones. To make a bouquet similar to the one shown in color above, you will need several sprays of snowballs, goldenrod, fern leaves (see page 620), zinnias, and black-eyed Susans. Development of the arrangement is illustrated in figure C.

First, prepare the container (photograph 14). Insert stems of snowballs and smaller goldenrod into foam at the center of the arrangement. The bouquet now resembles figure C1. Place larger sprays of goldenrod to outline the shape of the arrangement (figure C2). The rule of thumb for a traditional arrangement like this is that the height of the arrangement should be twice the height of the container, and the width one and a half times its height.

Place zinnias and ferns next (figure C3). These are the smaller flowers and foliage that help fill the inside spaces of the arrangement.

Finish by placing the black-eyed Susans. These are the largest, most striking flowers of the arrangement; they should be added last and should be placed to catch and direct the eye.

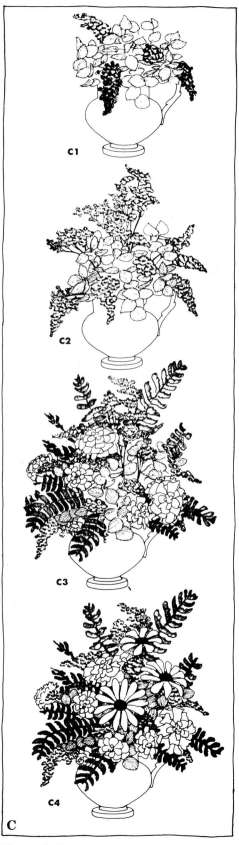

C1

C2

C3

C4

C

Figure C: Steps in making an arrangement. 619

The natural, delicate green of these dried maidenhair-fern fronds was kept by the pressing method of drying described below.

Air-Drying

The air-drying method of preserving herbs and flowers was practiced by the ancient Greeks, Romans, and people of the Middle Ages. It is simple—just strip plants of their leaves and hang them upside down in a dark, dry place (photograph 15). A great variety of flowers can be dried this way, including everlastings, celosia (crested and plume), baby's-breath, and globe thistle. Wild flowers include goldenrod, pearly everlasting, boneset, and dock. During country rambles, keep your eyes open for berries, seed pods, grasses, gnarly roots, and other low-moisture found supplies that can be air-dried.

Preserving with Glycerin

Although glycerin darkens and sometimes changes the color of the leaves, it lets them retain their shape, pliability, and texture (photograph 16). Buy glycerin at a drugstore, and prepare a solution of one part glycerin to three parts warm water. Cut two 1- or 2-inch slashes at the stem ends of the branches (photograph 17), and stand them in a glass jar filled with the solution. Add more solution as the original supply is absorbed. Soaking time required ranges from three days to three weeks or more, depending on the branch size. As soon as the uppermost leaves darken, remove the branches from the jar, and hang them upside down in a dark, dry place.

Foliage that can be preserved successfully with glycerin includes broadleaf evergreens, such as mountain laurel, Juliana barberry, and magnolia; needled evergreens, such as the yews; and branches of deciduous trees and shrubs, such as beech, apple, flowering crab, forsythia, and blueberry.

Pressing

Drying foliage by pressing it—with a weight, not an iron—between layers of paper is suitable for individual leaves, small branches, and ferns. This method preserves much of the original color; summer leaves remain green, and autumn leaves retain their brilliance. Keep the foliage fresh, and coat leaves with cooking oil on a soft cloth before pressing them. This will make them more pliable when dry. Place between several sheets of newspaper; cover with cardboard; weight with heavy objects. The cardboard distributes the weight. You can also press foliage in a telephone book (photograph 18). Drying time is two to four weeks, depending on thickness of the foliage.

Air-dried mangrove roots and oyster shells show the range of found supplies suitable for use in dried arrangements.

15: Hang weeds, flowers, and leaves in bunches upside down to air-dry. Use rubber bands for bunching. They will contract and remain tight as stems shrink. Fan out flowers in each bunch so they will not be flattened by crowding.

16: These magnolia leaves were preserved with glycerin. They remain shiny, resilient, and natural in shape. Be careful not to saturate such foliage. If top leaves begin to darken, absorption is sufficient; remove from solution.

To enlarge your views on effects that can be achieved with dried materials, here are a dried pomegranate, two dried Osage oranges, and fresh Osage oranges (the green ones). Dry them slowly in the oven at the lowest temperature setting.

17: Cut slashes with garden clippers at the stem ends of woody branches so the glycerin solution can be absorbed easily. Use a glass jar for the solution so you can see the level of the liquid. Add more solution as the level falls.

18: For pressing foliage, such as these maple leaves, separate the leaves as much as possible, and place them between pages of the telephone book. Close the book, and stack more books, or other heavy objects, on it to weight it down.

Look long enough at this arrangement of seashore finds, and you will hear waves crashing in the distance. Most plants that live by the sea dry quickly because they contain a minimum of moisture. They can be air-dried with great success.

Pine cones, kaffir corn, weeds, and grasses make up this farmer's-field arrangement. You can find these dried by nature or gather them fresh and air-dry.

621

Greenery and Growing Things
Dried-spice bouquet

Hans Koch was born in Germany, where, as a boy, he learned to make spice bouquets. He studied at the Academy of Arts of both Hamburg and Munich and now lives in New York City, where he has a textile-design business.

The miniature bouquet shown in the color photograph opposite is made with dried seeds, spices, and nuts and is delightfully scented. The flowers here are made by clustering various seeds and spices around nut centers. These are not intended to be copies of real flowers, but are creations of the imagination. Each cluster is formed at the end of a wire stem. The wires, 8 to 10 inches long, are gathered at the bouquet's center and secured with more wire. This mass of wire will be hidden by the container. The following instructions tell you how I made this bouquet; but once you have become familiar with the basic technique, you can improvise your own designs.

For color, I used dried baby's-breath and pink statice, but you can use any delicate, colorful dried flowers you have on hand. The dried spices I used were rosemary, dill weed, peppercorns, whole bay leaves, vanilla beans, cinnamon sticks, juniper berries, and whole cloves. I also used pumpkin, poppy, sesame, and caraway seeds; the meat and shells of hazelnuts, almonds, walnuts, pecans, and chestnuts; lentils, coffee beans, and dried corn kernels. Perhaps you grow some of these. If not, all are available at gourmet and health-food shops. You will probably have to buy more of each than you need to make a bouquet—a jar of each spice, for instance—but they are all nonperishable and can become stock for your larder. A spool of 28-gauge wire, wire cutters, a pair of pliers, small scissors or tweezers, and a tube of clear glue are also needed.

Arrange equipment, nuts, and mounds of spices and seeds on your worktable (photograph 19) for convenient dipping. I used shelled hazelnuts as the base for most of the flowers in the pictured bouquet. Loop wire around a nut, and twist the wire tightly to hold it. Leave a generous length of wire stem (at least 8 inches). Spread glue over the nut and dip the nut into one of the small seeds or spices. These will adhere to the glue-covered nut. Cover again with glue, and redip. Set aside to dry. Use the nuts in the arrangement as they are, or add to them in one of these ways:

Wrap whole cloves with wire, and form a circle of them around the seed-covered nut (photograph 21).

Glue a circle of corn-kernel, juniper-berry, or peppercorn petals around the nut. Or make two rows of petals; for instance, glue a circle of juniper berries and, directly below that, a circle of corn kernels.

Glue a circle of pumpkin seeds around the nut so that they resemble the petals of a daisy.

Glue pieces of walnut or pecan meat around the nut.

19: Assemble and organize seeds, spices, and equipment to make working with these very small ingredients easier. Here, glue-dipped sesame seeds on a hazelnut base are ready for a second coat of seeds.

20: Dip wired and glue-covered hazelnut into dill weed. When the nut is completely covered with the weed, shape it into a ball with the palm of your hand, and set it aside to dry.

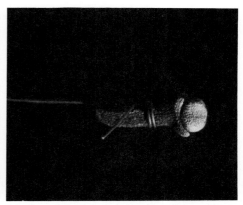

21: This is a close-up of a wired clove. Place cloves around a hazelnut; gather wires; twist around nut wire. Use this technique for coffee beans and ½-inch pieces of cinnamon stick or vanilla bean.

Cut vanilla beans or cinnamon sticks to ½-inch pieces; thread with wire, and form a circle of them around the nut.

Use whole, unshelled walnuts, pecans, and chestnuts as they are, without any decoration. Make a small hook at the end of a length of wire, and work it into the shell or the crack formed by the shell halves. Make more flowers by gluing lentils or coffee beans to the nutshell (photograph 22).

Wire bay leaves (photograph 23), and add them to the bouquet as foliage. Wire cinnamon sticks and whole vanilla beans (photograph 24), and attach them so they form spiky accents extending beyond the flower mass (color photograph below). The final step is the addition of real dried flowers, such as the pink statice and baby's-breath in this bouquet.

For related projects and crafts, see the entries "Ikebana," "Oshibana," "Pressed Flowers," and "Wild Flowers and Weeds."

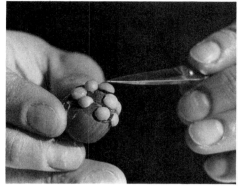

22: Glue lentils or coffee beans one by one to the nutshell. First, cover the shell with glue. Pick up each lentil or bean with the points of small scissors or with tweezers, and position it. Lentils and coffee beans should be glued with their flat sides down.

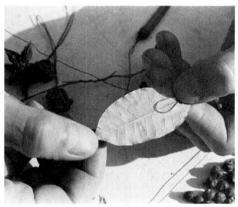

23: To wire a bay leaf, form a loop at the end of a length of wire, and fasten the loop to the underside of the leaf with transparent tape. Place several wired leaves at the base of the spice-and-seed arrangement, radiating them from the center, to support the bouquet.

Using dried seeds, spices, nuts, and flowers to make miniature bouquets like this is tradition of Austria, especially in the area around Salzburg. The vase is from the Biedermeier period, when this kind of bouquet was first made.

24: To wire a cinnamon stick, thread wire through the stick. Bend the wire end into a hook, and pull it back onto stick to hold it securely. The same technique is used on vanilla beans, which are long and hooked at one end. Insert wire into the straight end, which is open.

623

DULCIMERS
Strings for Folk Songs

Richard Manley teaches woodworking and dulcimer construction at the Craft Students League *in New York City. A graduate engineer and a one-time computer installer and programmer, his love of woodworking and music led him to change careers and establish his own business of building dulcimers and other stringed instruments. He assembles and sells his fine, handcrafted musical instruments in suburban Croton-On-Hudson, New York.*

There is nothing more rewarding than to be able to build something that is both beautiful to look at and beautiful to listen to. Remember the childhood fun of making objects that produced sounds—a musical comb or a willow whistle, for instance? The step beyond that—making something that will produce real music—is an even more satisfactory pastime.

Music is an essential part of everyday life, and this was demonstrated by the first settlers of the Appalachian Mountain region, who sought to make music in the American wilderness as they had in their native countries. There was room only for necessities in the small ships crossing to the new land, so few musical instruments could be brought along. But the settlers did bring memories of the European folk instruments that brightened their lives, and as a result of their attempts to reconstruct these instruments, the Appalachian dulcimer was born.

The word dulcimer is a combination of the Latin *dulce* ("sweet") and the Greek *melos* ("song" or "strain"). A stringed instrument of that name is mentioned in Syrian writings that date from 3000 B.C., but all we know about this instrument is that it was long, narrow, and had three strings. The Appalachian dulcimer at left is a descendant and a consolidation of four European folk instruments—the German *scheitholt*, the French *epinette des Vosges*, the Norwegian *langeleik*, and the Dutch *humle*. All of these were long, narrow stringed instruments that were played held horizontally on the lap or on a table. The first American dulcimers were box-shape, but gradually a violin-like hourglass shape and a teardrop shape (left) became predominant.

The dulcimer is popular today for the same reasons that it caught on when it first was made in America hundreds of years ago: It is easy to play, it is small and transportable, and it provides the right sound to accompany traditional ballads. Dulcimers are sold at relatively low cost in kit or finished form, but if you like working with wood, build your own. It can be any of a number of shapes, of any kind of wood, have whatever shape sound holes you like, and have three, four, or more strings. In other words, it can be personalized in different ways, without any appreciable effect on the sound. The toy dulcimer in the project that follows is a strung fret board without a sound box, yet it sounds as authentic, when played on a carton or table, as a real dulcimer. For this project, the frets, (metal wires against which the playing string is pressed to change a note) are staples driven into the fretboard.

Front view (at the left) and side view (above) of a dulcimer are pictured here to show details of this unusual instrument. Looking at the front view the top is the nut end and the bottom is the bridge end. The string on the far left is the melody string, and the other two are drone strings that are kept at fixed pitches and give the dulcimer's sound its unusual quality. To make this dulcimer, see page 626.

Performing Arts

Fretboard dulcimer

Making a toy dulcimer (right) will familiarize you with some of the mechanics of building a real one (page 626), and will give you the opportunity to learn to play a dulcimer without a great investment of time and energy.

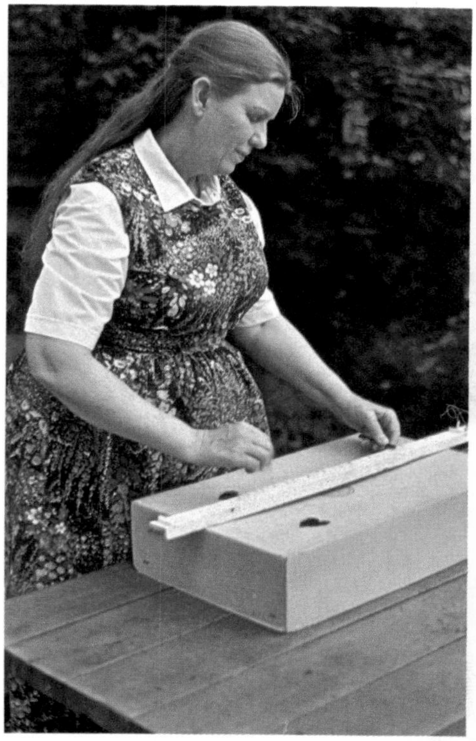

Jean Ritchie, born in Viper, Kentucky, is a well-known dulcimer performing artist. Her ancestors, of Scotch-Irish origins, have been filling Kentucky's Cumberland Mountains with the sound of the dulcimer for generations. Now a resident of Long Island, N.Y., Miss Ritchie is the author of Singing Family of the Cumberlands *and* The Dulcimer Book. *Here she plays the children's dulcimer that she designed. The cardboard box performs somewhat the same function as the sound box on a real dulcimer. The sound holes are cut in a traditional heart shape.*

Materials and Tools

I used found materials where possible. These include two small pieces of wood ⅛-by-⅜-by-1½ inches for the two string supports (they can be cut from a piece of scrap wood, an old ruler, or a piece of wood molding); three wood screws to anchor the strings at one end; a large cardboard carton, visible in the photograph at right, to act as a sound box; and, to play the dulcimer, a popsicle stick for a noter, and a wedge cut from a plastic food storage container top for a pick. Articles you will need to purchase are: A 30-inch piece of 1-by-2-inch trimmed hardwood lumber; three autoharp or harpsichord tuning pegs; and a set of three dulcimer strings. The dulcimer strings can be purchased at a music shop and so can the tuning pegs, although they may be more difficult to find. If you have difficulty locating any, you can order them by mail from Zuckerman Harpsichords Inc., 160 Avenue of the Americas, New York, N. Y.

Tools you will need are a ruler and pencil, a crosscut handsaw, medium-texture sandpaper, a heavy-duty staple gun and staples, a hammer, a screwdriver, a hand or power drill with a 3/16 bit for drilling wood, and a pair of slip-joint pliers for turning the tuning pegs.

Getting Started

Place the 1-by-2-by-30 inch board on your work table, and with ruler and pencil, mark a line across board width 1⅞ inches from one end and another line 2 inches from the same end. These two lines, ⅛ inches apart, outline the groove that will be cut for one of the string supports. This will be the tuning-peg end, and the string support at this end is called the nut.

With ruler, measure down fretboard from line drawn 2 inches from end, and mark off fret points (photograph 1, and table below). Mark two lines ½ inch and ⅝ inch from tail end of board (opposite tuning-peg end). These lines outline the groove for the bridge (tail-end string support).

Cut the small pieces of wood for bridge and nut. Both should measure ⅛-by-⅜-by-1⅝ inches. Cut three saw-cut wide, diagonal notches for strings into one edge of the top of the nut. Notches should be ⅛-inch deep and cut into outer top edge of nut at about 45 degrees; inner top edge is not notched. Locate one notch at mid-point of the 1⅝-inch length of the nut, and the

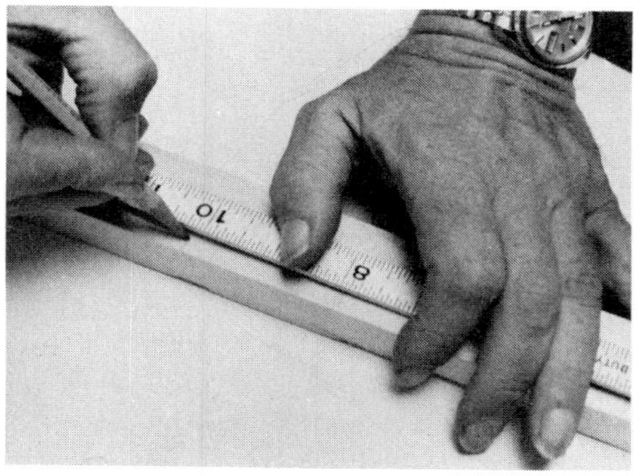

1: Using a ruler and pencil, mark off the fret points near the edge of the board with small lines. Measure from the inside edge of the nut and follow the measurements in the table at the right.

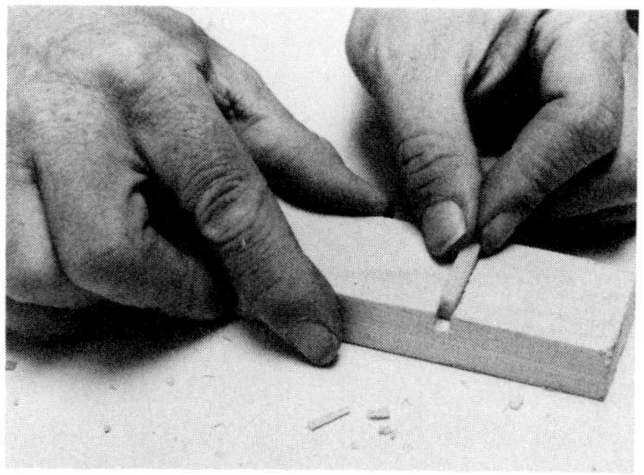

2: Fit the nut into its slot. If you were careful not to make groove wider than ⅛ inch, the nut will fit tightly and require hand pressure to insert all the way. Put bridge in place in the same manner.

FRET MEASUREMENTS:
Distance, in inches,
from near edge of nut
to center of each fret:

1	3	9	16¾
2	5⅝	10	17¼
3	6⅞	11	18½
4	9⅛	12	19½
5	11¼	13	19⅞
6	12⅛	14	20¾
7	13⅞	15	21½
8	15⅝		

other two ⅜ inch in from either end. The bridge is not notched.

Set bridge and nut aside and go back to fret board. With saw held in horizontal position, cut grooves for nut and bridge. For each groove, first make two saw cuts ³/₁₆-inch deep just inside the two pencil marks. Then saw in between until groove is ⅛-inch wide and ³/₁₆-inch deep. Press nut and bridge into their grooves (photograph 2). If groove is too tight, sand it with sandpaper wrapped around popsicle stick. Glue is not needed if cut is exact.

Insert screws for anchoring strings, and add frets (see photographs 3 and 4). Next, drill holes for the three tuning pegs and insert pegs as shown in photograph 5. To string, tune and play the fret board, see the next to the last paragraph on page 633 and the Craftnotes on page 632.

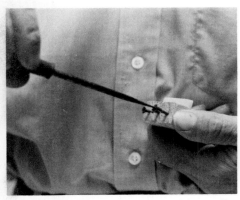

3: Make pilot holes for screws with a nail, then insert screws with screwdriver. Place screws roughly the same distance from each other as are the string notches in the nut. Let screws protrude ¼ inch.

4: Center a staple on one of each penciled fret mark (see photograph 1, page 625). Position them along board edge nearest you when nut end is at your left. Staples will lie beneath melody string.

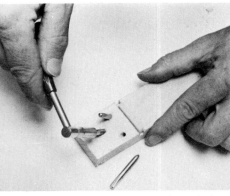

5: After drilling holes for the threaded tuning pegs, screw pegs into the board until they begin to come out the other side. A tuning wrench is being used here, but a pair of pliers will also work.

The outdoors is the dulcimer's concert hall. Miss Ritchie is playing an old teardrop dulcimer. The Ritchie family has preserved and passed on many English ballads (Barbry Ellen, Lord Randal) well-suited to the dulcimer's plaintive sound.

Performing Arts
Appalachian dulcimer

To make the teardrop-shape dulcimer pictured on page 624, it helps to have woodworking skill. But a beginner, being very careful about measuring, sawing and fitting, can manage the project if he allows plenty of time for it. Only hand tools are required, and your neighbor may be able to supply you with those you don't have. The tools needed are: A metal ruler calibrated to thirty-secondths of an inch; adjustable T-square; wood vise; plane; saw; five or six C-clamps; jigsaw; fine rasp; rattail file; drill with ⁹/₁₆, ½, ⁷/₃₂ and ¹/₁₆ inch bits; mat knife; thin-blade dovetail saw or fret saw; wire cutters; hammer; protractor; and small paintbrush.

For the dulcimer parts shown opposite, you will need two 32-inch pieces of 1-by-6 and one 16-inch piece of 1-by-4 hardwood lumber; it can be cherry, birch, walnut, mahogany or maple. Other materials needed: A good supply of No. 80 (coarse) and No. 120 (fine) sandpaper; palm-size block of cork; large bottle of white glue; scrap wood for bracing and clamping; ¾-inch thick plywood board 29½ by 8 inches; one sheet of carbon paper and one of tracing paper; masking tape; four 2½-inch finishing (no head) nails; three ⅜-inch roundhead brass nails; thirty ½-inch nails; linseed oil and turpentine. The instrument parts needed are three guitar tuning-gear assemblies with 1¹/₆-inch shafts and screws for fastening (see photograph 29, page 633); two feet (or, if already cut, 17 1¼-inch pieces) of guitar fret wire; and a set of three dulcimer strings. The instrument parts (and the fret saw if you don't have one or a thin-blade dovetail saw) can be purchased at music stores that repair stringed instruments. Or, if you can't find them there, you can order them from a catalog obtainable from H.L. Wild, 510 E. 11th St., New York, N.Y. 10009.

Basic Assembly

In brief, the dulcimer is assembled as follows: The lumber is cut for fret board, front, sides, and back; the front, side and back pieces are split; back pieces are glued together; lumber for neck is cut to size and split; neck pieces are glued together, and cut out; tail block is cut out; sides are shaped and glued to tail and neck; fret board is fastened to front pieces; back and front are glued to sides, and then back and front overhang is cut off along side curves. Follow this detailed procedure:

Cutting Wood for the Fret Board and the Sound Box

The first step is to saw the fret board and the front, side, and back pieces shown in figure A, below. Saw one 32-inch piece of 1-by-6 into two widths, one 3¾-inches wide from which the back pieces will be cut, and the other 1¼-inches wide for the fret board. Saw the second 32-inch piece of 1-by-6 into two widths, one 3¼-inches wide from which the front pieces will be cut, the other 1¾-inches wide from which the sides will be cut. Set the fret-board piece aside for the present. Save excess for cutting nut and bridge.

Now rule a line down the center of the ¾-inch thickness (a purchased 1-by-6 is actually ¾-by-5⅝, of course) of each of the remaining three pieces. Saw through each to split it into two thinner pieces of same length and width (photograph 6). Or have this done where wood is purchased; make sure it is understood wood must be split exactly down middle. You will now have three pairs of wood pieces. Label sawn and unsawn sides and where each piece is to be used. Sawn surfaces will face inside finished dulcimer. Clamp one piece at a time to your work table and plane sawn side to a thickness of ⅛ to ³⁄₁₆ inch. Always put piece of scrap wood between clamps and good wood. Plane with grain, away from clamp; change clamp to other end and finish operation. Sand planed surfaces with #80 sandpaper wrapped around cork block (cork has just the right consistency to make a good hardwood sanding block). After sanding, always wipe sanded surfaces with a soft dry cloth. Put aside the pieces for the front and the sides.

6: Saw through board's ¾-inch thickness as shown to make thin wood for sound box. Stop periodically to move board up. Put scrap wood between vise and good wood.

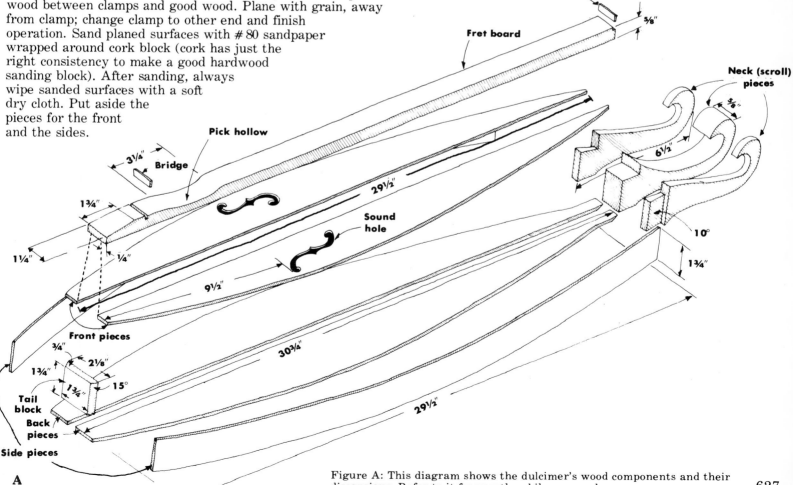

Figure A: This diagram shows the dulcimer's wood components and their dimensions. Refer to it frequently while you work.

A

7: Place back pieces one on top of the other (sawn sides out and grain patterns matching). Plane edges simultaneously. When planing, hold pieces in place with clamped scrap-wood pieces, as shown.

8: Wait five minutes after joining pieces, and remove excess glue with end of scrap-wood stick. Do this every time you glue. Also, put cloth or wax paper underneath so pieces do not stick to work table.

Gluing Pieces for the Back

Hold back pieces together so grain patterns on unsawn sides match. Plane edges that will be joined (see figure A, previous page, and photograph 7) until they fit together smoothly. Sand with block and No. 120 paper. Apply glue to both edges and smooth with fingers. Rub boards together to further distribute glue, and with unsawn surfaces up, clamp firmly together. Remove excess glue. If boards don't lie flat, clamp scrap board on top (photograph 9). When glue has set (about one hour), remove boards and sand seam on both sides with cork-block sander—first with No. 80 paper, then No. 120.

Making the Neck

The neck piece (scroll) is a three-piece wood sandwich (see figure B opposite). Cut the 16-inch piece of 1-by-4 into two 6½-inch lengths. Save (for dulcimer's tail block) the 3-inch piece left over. Make outer two neck pieces by splitting one of the 6½-inch pieces into two ⅜-inch-thick pieces. Plane each on sawn sides to $5/16$-inch thickness. Sand with cork-block sander and No. 80 paper. The other 6½-inch length is for neck's middle piece. Do not split it, but plane it to a thickness of ⅝ inches. Sand with sander.

With tracing paper, trace all solid and dotted lines, including hole crosses, of neck pattern (figure C, page 630). Then place this tracing-paper pattern, with carbon paper underneath, onto one side of ⅝-inch-thick block. Line up block edges with dotted pattern edges, and retrace dotted line shown in red in pattern (figure C). Lift paper and carbon; line should be on wood.

Place block in vise and cut along carbon line with jigsaw to remove U-shape section of wood. Save it. File and sand cut (photograph 10). To join scroll outer pieces to inner piece, and to finish cutting, follow the directions of photographs 11, 12, and 13. File and sand sawn surfaces as was done on inner piece (photograph 10). Then turn over tracing-paper pattern and, with carbon, transfer the dotted line hole crosses to the other side of the cut-out scroll. Be sure, when doing this, that scroll pattern edges are lined up with actual scroll edges.

To drill the tuning-peg holes, use a $7/32$-inch bit. Mark off length of tuning-peg shaft (1$1/16$ inches) on your drill bit by wrapping bit with masking tape at a point 1⅛ inches from its tip. Discount cone-shape point of bit when measuring its length. Set neck in vise and push U-shape piece, cut out earlier, back in place between outer pieces of sandwich to prevent wood from splintering. To keep drill from slipping, first lightly hammer a starter hole with a nail where hole center lines cross. Then, stopping when you reach tape edge on bit, drill two holes on one side, turn block over, and drill one hole on other side. Drill will go through one outer piece and slightly penetrate other. Remove U-shape scrap and set neck aside until later.

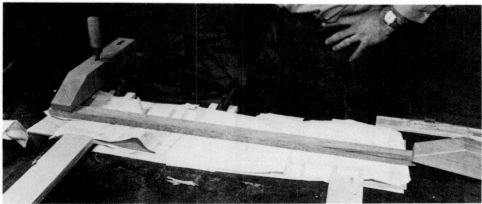

9: Hold boards of back, unsawn sides up, in jig of clamps and scrap wood. If they won't lie flat, clamp scrap piece on top, as shown. Always, before gluing, test by placing the pieces to be glued in clamps and scrap wood to make sure the arrangement works.

10: Smooth jigsaw cut in center block at neck (see text above) with rounded side of a rasp. Smooth cut further with No. 120 sandpaper wrapped around rasp.

11: Glue and clamp three scroll pieces together (see figure B). Align bottom and sides. Let glue set. Remove clamps and file bottom and sides flush.

12: Transfer solid lines and hole crosses of traced pattern (page 630), with carbon, to one side of scroll block. Align dotted line with inside-piece cut.

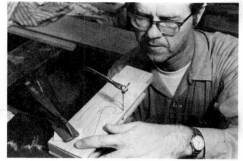

13: To cut out scroll, saw along solid lines of pattern with a jigsaw, with block clamped. You will have to remove clamp and re-clamp as you saw each section.

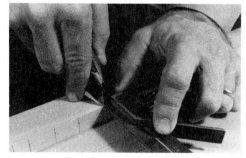

14: Measure from near edge of nut notch, and mark frets (see table, right) on tape stuck to board side. Holding T-square to mark, cut across top with mat knife.

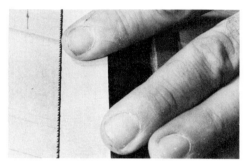

15: Mark fret-wire depth on fret saw with masking tape. Cross-section view of wire is T-shape. Measure depth of ridge that forms T bottom ($1/16$-inch) and tape on saw.

16: Align T-square with knife cut, and saw fret notches up to tape on saw. Make sure cut is to full depth of distance marked so wire will sit snugly in groove.

Preparing the Fret Board

Take the 1¼-by-¾-by-32-inch fret board and cut its length to 29½ inches. With No. 80 paper, plane and sand its ¾-inch depth to a depth of ⅝ inches. Use this planed surface as the back of the fret board. Sand sides with No. 120 paper. Rule a pencil line across board width ⅛ inch from one end to mark edge of notch where nut will fit (see figure A, page 627). To measure, mark and cut the 17 fret-wire notches, follow steps in photographs 14 through 16.

After cutting fret notches, rule two lines ⅛-inch apart to mark position of bridge (see measurements, right). Bridge and nut grooves both must be $3/16$-inch deep and ⅛-inch wide. Mark $3/16$-inch depth with tape on fret saw. For bridge groove, make two $3/16$-inch deep cuts at bridge pencil lines, and then make cuts in between until groove is complete. Nut groove is at board end and open on one side (see figure A, page 627); make one cut $3/16$-inch deep at pencil line and another at right angles to it ⅛-inch into board end. Sand both grooves with No. 120 paper wrapped around popsicle stick.

Draw a 3¼-inch long indentation, no deeper than ⅜ inch, on fretboard sides for pick hollow (see figure A). File and sand it out.

Finishing the Neck and Making the Tail Piece

Draw two lines on top of neck-piece end at 10-degree angles from corners (use protractor, and see figure D1 on following page and figure A, page 627). Do the same on bottom and saw into neck along these lines. Then cut into both sides of neck, to free the two wedge-shape pieces shown as red areas in figure D1. The dulcimer sides will fit into these triangular recesses.

To make tail block, take the 3-inch piece of 1-by-4 (actually ¾-by-3½) left when originally cutting wood for neck, and cut out a piece measuring 1¾-by-¾-by-2⅛ inches from the middle of its 3½-inch length. Use

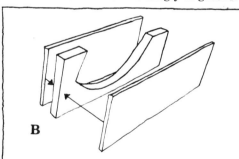

B

Figure b: Split wood forms outer pieces of neck sandwich. U-shape is cut from the middle piece before gluing.

FRET MEASUREMENTS:
Distance, in inches, from near edge of nut to center of each fret and edges of bridge:

1	$2^{27}/_{32}$	11	$17^{13}/_{16}$
2	$5^{7}/_{16}$	12	$18^{25}/_{32}$
3	$6^{21}/_{32}$	13	$19^{1}/_{4}$
4	$8^{27}/_{32}$	14	$20^{1}/_{16}$
5	$10^{25}/_{32}$	15	$20^{25}/_{32}$
6	$11^{11}/_{16}$	16	$21^{7}/_{16}$
7	$13^{11}/_{32}$	17	$21^{3}/_{4}$
8	$14^{13}/_{16}$	near edge of bridge	$26^{27}/_{32}$
9	$16^{1}/_{8}$	far edge of bridge	$26^{31}/_{32}$
10	$16^{23}/_{32}$		

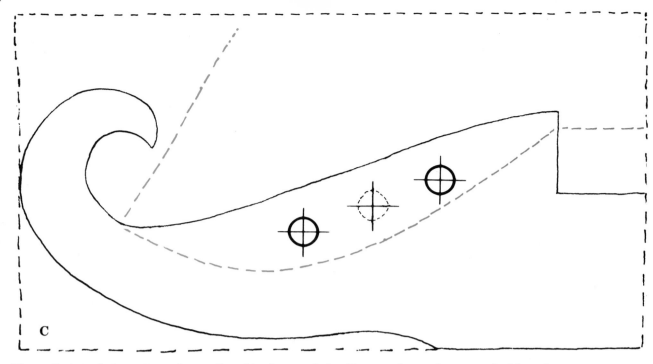

Figure C: Actual-size pattern for scroll and tuning-peg holes. Trace and transfer to wood with carbon.

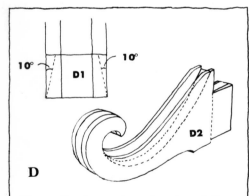

Figure D1: A top view of neck end. Saw along dotted lines. D2: Completed neck piece. Saw into straight dotted line on sides, to free wedge-shaped piece.

leftover end pieces later for clamping. Bevel the tail block according to measurements and angles in figure A, page 627. Then sand the bevels with No. 120 paper.

Use a plywood piece measuring 29½ by 8 inches as a frame on which to shape sides and glue them to neck and tail pieces. Rule a centerline down length of plywood. Center neck, face down (with L-shape notch on neck fitting around edge of board), at one end of line and tail block at other. Clamp both securely (see photograph 17). Rule another line crossing centerline at right angles at a point 12 inches from tail block. On cross line, 3 inches from centerline on each side, hammer a finishing nail to depth of about ½ inch (see photograph 17). Glue and clamp ends of sides to neck (photograph 18). Shape sides around nails and glue and clamp tail block (photograph 19). Leave in place and go on to the next step.

Cutting the Sound Holes and Finishing the Front
Cut both front pieces to 29½-inch lengths. Transfer pattern, figure E, for sound hole onto one of the front boards (see figure A, page 627). Position it

17: Place wax paper or cloth under neck and tail pieces to catch glue, and clamp both to plywood board. Hammer finishing nails, and test position of sides, as shown.

18: Apply glue, and clamp side pieces to neck bevel. Use two pieces of wood cut at 10-degree angles between clamps and sides. Be sure unsawn side surfaces face in.

so larger circular opening is an inch from one edge, smaller is ⅜ inch from
other edge, and larger is 9½ inches from tail block end. Align this board
on top of other front board, back to back, and clamp to scrap wood to keep
them from splintering when drilled. Drill larger sound hole circle with a
⁹/₁₆-inch bit and smaller with a ½ inch bit. Remove clamps and align the three
boards in your vise. Cut out rest of sound hole with jigsaw. To do this,
remove one end of saw blade from its frame, insert it through one of the
holes, and attach it to frame again. Smooth cut edges with rattail file, and

19: Apply glue to other end of sides,
bend around nails, and clamp to tail, as
shown. Use pieces sawn off when making
tail, as scrap between clamp and sides.

20: Glue front boards to fret board.
Before glue sets, hammer ½-inch nails at
2-inch intervals along edges of both
front boards. Keep boards aligned at ends.

21: Lightly hammer the pieces of fret
wire, toothed-ridge down, into the
notches on fret board. Use scrap wood
between hammer and wire, to protect wire.

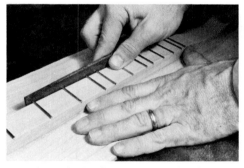

22: When all the fret wires are in place,
file both ends with flat side of the rasp
until flush with fret-board sides. Then
file tips at 45-degree angle to finish.

23: For accurate sanding of side edges,
use a sanding board made of scrap board
and some No. 80 sandpaper. Attach the
sandpaper to the board with white glue.

then sand with file wrapped with No. 80 paper. Be careful not to bevel edges.
    To attach front boards to fret board, place fret board, back side up, on
work table. On both sides of it, place pieces of scrap wood the same thickness
as the fret board. Rest the two front boards on these, planed side up, so they
are lined up lengthwise at both sides of fret board, and each overlaps the fret
board ¼ inch. Make sure pick hollow of fret board and larger circles of
sound holes on front boards are both closer to the tail end, and that smaller
sound-hole circles are the ones closest to the fret board (see figure A, page
627). Glue and nail front boards to fret board (see photograph 20). When glue
has set, turn over front assembly, sand fret-board top, and round edges
slightly with block sander and No. 120 paper. File and sand a slight incline
on 1¾ inches of fret-board tail end (see photograph 26, page 632).

Fastening the Back and the Front to the Sides
Unlike any of the previous steps in the assembly of the dulcimer, the two
steps of gluing the back and then gluing the front to the sides must be done
on the same day to avoid warping. First, place one or two 6-inch lengths of
scrap wood at points where they will fit snugly between the two sides still

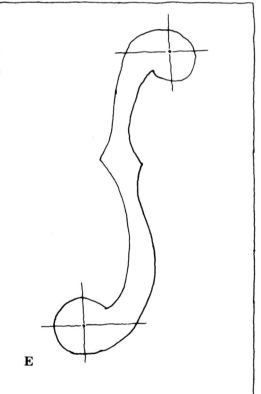

E

Figure E: Trace this pattern, including hole
crosses, and transfer to wood with carbon.

631

DULCIMER CRAFTNOTES

Tuning and Playing the Dulcimer.
By turning the tuning pegs, tune the first and second strings to G above middle C and the third string to middle C, itself. You can use a piano or pitch pipe, but if you have neither of these, tune your dulcimer by ear. Tighten the third string until it is under a fair amount of tension. With your left-hand thumb, press the string onto the fret board to the left of the fourth fret (count from the tuning peg end placed at your left). Pluck the string with your right hand. The pitch you hear is what the first and second strings should be tuned to.

The proper way of playing the dulcimer is to sit on a fairly low stool or chair, and rest the instrument on your lap with the scroll to your left (see photograph 30, opposite). The noter (a 3 to 4-inch length of narrow bamboo cut from a garden stake or a popsicle stick) is used to change the pitch of the melody string only. Hold it between the thumb and forefinger of your left hand and rest the end of it on the first string, with the side of your forefinger against the side of the fret board. This will enable you to slide the noter up and down the melody string without touching the second string.

With the noter, press the melody string to the left of the third fret. Pluck the string with your right hand; the note you hear is C. To play the scale of C Major, pluck the melody string, as you slide the noter up to each successive fret, stopping at the tenth (press the strings just to the left of each fret for the best sound). Do this again, but instead of plucking the melody string only, strum all the strings with a pick in your right hand, while sliding the noter to each fret, as above.

For an ideal pick, cut a rounded triangle out of the top of a plastic food storage container. You can use a guitar pick, but they're a bit too stiff for smooth dulcimer playing.

A turkey or goose quill is the traditional pick (see photograph of Miss Ritchie, page 626).

Play the scale up and down until you feel comfortable with the instrument, and then try to pick out some simple tunes. For further information about tuning, and for some music to play, see *The Dulcimer Book* by Jean Ritchie, Oak Publications, 33 W. 60th St., New York, N.Y. 10023.

24: After applying glue to the side pieces and the back piece, clamp them in place, as shown. Clamp the neck and tail ends first and then clamp the sides.

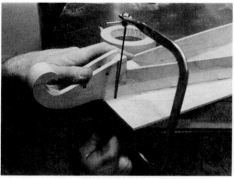

25: Saw off the back-piece overhang as close to the sides as possible without touching. Also saw off overhang of the side pieces at the tail end, and front piece, when attached. Sand small remaining overhang flush with sides.

26: Hammer the nails that will secure the strings into the incline on the tail end of fret board. Place in any pattern, as long as each lines up along fret board with one of the notches in the nut. They should protrude 3/16 inch.

clamped to frame (see photograph 24). Fashion a sanding board to sand side edges (see photograph 23, previous page). Remove clamps from one end to sand it, replace and then remove from other end. Do not remove nails from frame.

Take the assembled piece for dulcimer back and saw it to a length of 30¾ inches. Lift dulcimer side, ends, and rib supports in one piece off nails and frame. Place back board, planed side up, onto some scrap wood supports and rest dulcimer assembly scroll up, on top of it (see photograph 24). Center it and align tail piece with one end and beginning of curve on neck bottom with other end. As a guide for gluing, trace around side edges. Replace in position, clamp until glue sets, then saw as in photograph 25. Clamp and sand top edges of side pieces with sanding board as before. Glue front assembly to sides in same manner that back was glued (see above), with the exception that front is glued *down* onto sides. Clamp and let glue set. Remove clamps, saw off overhang, and then plane back and front edges. Sand them flush with sides with sanding block and No. 80 paper, then sand all over sound box with No. 120 paper to smooth surfaces and round edges slightly.

Applying Finish
Dulcimers traditionally are not finished as painstakingly as other stringed instruments are. Boiled linseed oil is all that is needed to preserve the wood and give it a rich patina. Brush on a mixture of half turpentine and half linseed oil for first application. Soak 30 minutes and wipe dry. Additional coats of straight boiled linseed oil may be applied until desired sheen is reached. Wait 24 hours between coats, wiping dry 30 minutes after each coat has been applied.

27: For checking height of bridge, string distance above second fret should be thickness of match cover. If distance is too great or small, adjust bridge.

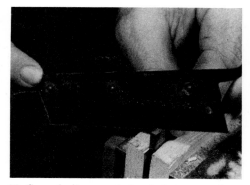

28: Saw shallow angled cuts into one edge of nut with the fret saw. Strings then will touch only a tiny area of the nut. This will assure accuracy of pitch.

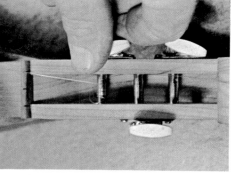

29: Wind each string around one of tuning shafts, as shown. Two pegs of one orientation lie in holes on one side, and one of opposite is in hole on other side.

Stringing the Dulcimer

Put the three tuning pegs in their proper holes in scroll (photograph 29). Mark places for their screws by tapping nail into screw holes while pegs are in place. Remove pegs and drill shallow holes with 1/16-inch bit to start screws. Replace pegs and fasten screws. I used brass nails for anchoring strings at the tail end of fret board (photograph 26 opposite) but any kind of small nail will do. To prevent splitting, start nails by drilling shallow holes with 1/16-inch bit, and then hammer in place.

Cut nut and bridge from leftover wood, and file both to 1¼-by-⅛-by-⅜-inch dimensions. Leave top of nut flat, but round top of bridge. Place bridge in its groove. No glue should be needed for either fret or bridge. They will fit tightly without it. Bridge should protrude about 3/16 inch above fret board, but check its height with one of the strings. Place string loop around one of the nails at tail-piece end, and extend it over bridge and along fret board up to first fret. Press it on first fret and check string clearance on second fret with unfolded match-book cover (photograph 27). If string is too high, file bridge. If too low, make bridge groove shallower with wood filler or put masking tape on bridge bottom. Keep string in place for testing nut.

With fret saw, cut three shallow angled slots in nut (photograph 28). Two outside slots should be ¼ inch in from nut's ends, and middle slot should be ⅜ inch away, on each side, from other slots. Put nut in place so higher sides of angled slots face away from scroll. Strings should touch this side of nut only. To determine proper depth of angled slots, take string still in place and extend it through one of nut slots. Rest it in slot and hold it, without pulling down on it. Make sure string clears first fret by at least the thickness of match-book cover. It is better to have string too high than too low above fret. But try to bring it as close to match-cover thickness as possible. Cut slot in nut deeper, as needed. Make sure angle of cut is great enough so that, when string is in place, it still rests only on side of nut away from scroll. Test other nut slots with remaining strings in same manner.

To string the dulcimer, lay it horizontally in front of you with the scroll to your left. The two thin wire strings of your set should be strung nearest you and the heavier string farthest away. This is the opposite of guitar-string placement. Loop each string on one of the nails at the tail end, and thread it through either of the holes in one of the tuning shafts at the other end (photograph 29). Turn tuning-peg handle so string wraps around shaft. Catch loose end in string being wound. Continue until string is taut. Cut off excess string with wire clippers. For tuning and playing, see the Craftnotes on the opposite page.

For related projects and crafts, see the entries "Musical Composition," "Whistles and Flutes," "Woodworking," and "Zithers."

30: Mr. Manly shows the correct way of playing. Your dulcimer will provide hours of enjoyment if you learn to play. It's as easy as playing piano with one finger.

EGG DECORATION
Jewels of Easter

For centuries, the egg has symbolized the mysteries of birth, death, and reawakening in the rites and pageants of spring. In the Early Christian church, the egg played a central role in many Easter customs and liturgical dramas celebrating the Resurrection of Christ. On Easter Sunday in Greece, people bang their red-dyed eggs against those of others saying, "Christ is risen," receiving the reply, "He is risen indeed." The popular custom of rolling colored eggs down slopes on Easter Monday probably originated in 19th century England. Also in England, at Chester Cathedral, the bishop and dean supposedly engaged in egg-tossing with the choir boys as the antiphon was sung on Easter Sunday. The tradition of coloring eggs may have its roots in a legend almost 2,000 years old. It is said that an egg merchant, Simon of Cyrene, helped to carry Christ's cross to Calvary. Having left his basket of eggs by the roadside, he was amazed to find them miraculously colored upon his return. Egg coloring developed into an art in the Slavic countries where, in the Ukraine, it is called *pysanka* and in Lithuania, *margutis*. Designs vary from geometric to animal or floral depending upon the region. But the method used is the same, a wax-resist technique of decorating that is similar to batik fabric dyeing. Though the tools and materials are simple, they produced the complex and beautiful designs pictured on the opposite page.

Kitchen Favorites and Celebrations
Margutis and pysanka eggs

Begin by selecting clean, unmarred eggs of any kind. Chicken eggs are of course the cheapest and most available, but craft shops stock (or know where to get) duck, turkey, emu, quail, and ostrich eggs. Some of these are speckled or colored, but their variations may simply be incorporated into your design. Eggs may be worked on raw or hard-boiled, or may be blown to remove the contents, to insure against messy breakage (something to consider if children will be handling them). I prefer not to blow those I decorate. It results in holes that may interfere with the design. But if you want to remove the contents, puncture each end with a pin or fine scissor point, and break the yoke by jabbing carefully through the hole. Then, holding the egg over a bowl, blow down through the top hole. Rinse the shell immediately under running water to prevent it from smelling. As you handle the egg, check frequently to see that your hands are clean, as even the natural oils from your skin may prevent the wax from adhering properly. To get a surface to which the dye will adhere better, wash the egg in yogurt and rinse well with cool water. (Vinegar or baking soda will also do the job.) Food dyes, which are harmless, cheap, and have bright colors, are probably your best bet. If children will be dyeing eggs, check when you buy dyes to make sure they do not contain aniline, which is toxic, and that they are not permanent colors, which will stain clothing.

You will need cups, one for each color; vinegar; pencils with erasers; several straight pins with various sized heads; and a candle or beeswax. Beeswax is preferable because it adheres better. It comes in blocks at craft shops, but it is cheaper to get it at a sewing store where it is sold (for waxing thread) in a one ounce package that will do a dozen eggs. Cover your work surface with newspaper to prevent stains from wax and dyes from spoiling table tops.

Mix the dyes according to the directions on the labels. Add two tablespoons of vinegar to each pint of coloring to promote a consistent distribution of color over the egg. Be sure that dyes of any kind are completely cold before immersing eggs, since heat might melt the wax off the eggs.

Sandra Cipkas works with the wax-resist method of dyeing eggs that she learned in her native Lithuania as a child. There, this technique is called margutis. *In her home just outside Baltimore, Sandra paints, does needlepoint, and makes rugs. She formerly was a professional dancer.*

Colored eggs were dyed with a wax-resist technique known as *margutis* to Lithuanians and *pysanka* in the Ukraine. The floral motifs on these eggs are characteristic of Lithuania.

EGG-DYEING CRAFTNOTES

Homemade dyes: It is easy to make your own natural dyes the way it was done before the proliferation of synthetics. Onionskin produces one of the oldest kinds of homemade dye, yielding a range of colors from yellow through orange, red, and brown, to near-black. An old recipe requires that you boil a quantity of onionskins in enough water to cover them. The color produced depends upon how long you boil the skins and the length of time you leave the egg in the dye. People of the Middle East and Europe also use coffee and natural dyes extracted from barks and berries for staining eggshells.

Patterns and Processes

In selecting your design for *margutis* or *pysanka* eggs, you can use any of the traditional floral Slavic designs shown in the accompanying photographs. Or, among some of the most popular are the Christian symbols of the cross or fish, fertility symbols such as ears of wheat, pairs of deer or horses, the sun, and the tree of life. Many of the patterns found on *margutis* eggs are also taken from traditional embroidery. It might help to work out your design first on paper with a pencil to make sure that what you plan to put on the egg will fit into the space available. But don't draw on the egg with a pencil; the graphite will show through the dye and cannot be erased after waxing. In working out your design, remember that you will apply wax to those areas you don't want dyed, which is why this is called a wax-resist method. Successive dyeings should go from lighter to darker colors and it helps to plan that sequence in advance.

Waxing

If you decide to use beeswax, melt it over a low heat in a double boiler (never over a direct flame) or in a small chafing dish with a candle underneath. Hot wax is combustible; use a thermometer to make sure the temperature of the wax does not rise above 300 degrees Fahrenheit. Stick the various-sized pinheads into the erasers of the pencils; these are your stylus tools. When the candle has formed a pool, or the beeswax is melted, dip the pinhead into the wax and stroke it quickly

1: A candle-heated chafing dish warms beeswax to a workable consistency while keeping the temperature low.

2: Styluses made of pencils and pins are simple but effective tools that can produce a variety of effects.

along the egg. If you have picked up too much wax on the pinhead, stroke it across your thumbnail before marking the egg. Use a small pinhead for fine lines and ball-headed pins for wider ones. If the line starts to skip, the wax is not hot enough. To increase the temperature of the candle wax, heat the pinhead directly in the flame for a moment before picking up the wax. Give yourself time to get used to the feel of the stylus and wax. Use a rubberband stretched around the egg as a guide for longer lines. Be careful not to cover large areas with wax at one time as it may come off during dyeing.

Once you have applied a wax pattern to the egg and the wax has cooled, put the egg into its first dye bath. If you had planned to dye an egg more than one color, you will have left space in your design for the second or third waxing. Put as many colors on as you want but, to obtain the truest color in a series of dyeings, the sequence must be from light to dark, (for example, yellow, orange, red, green, blue, purple). Any of these hues applied over another will acquire a slight tint from the one beneath, something useful to know if you decide to alter the above order. Check the color every few minutes until you are satisfied with the shade; then remove the egg from the dye with tongs or a spoon, place it on paper towelings and let dry. Do not rub or pat dry with toweling or the dye will come off. If you leave the first wax on, that area will remain white in the final design. If, however, you want the second color to adhere in the areas covered by the first waxing, remove the wax by holding the egg over low heat with tongs (not too near) and wipe frequently with dry paper towels. Never scrape wax off and do not

A

Figure A: Stroke the egg with the side of the pinhead to make tapering lines. The line thins because the wax on the pin is used up quickly.

use cleansers; these will remove the dye. Apply the wax over areas you don't want redyed to preserve the first color during the next dyeing.

To cover mistakes, or to add some localized color, you can "spot dye" with a small paintbrush. You can also create an etched effect by scratching a design through the dye with a pin. When the egg is completed to your satisfaction melt off the wax over low heat or in an oven set at 150 degrees Fahrenheit for 15 minutes. Do not use a candle flame; the carbon from it will discolor the egg. Give your finished egg a gloss by rubbing it with a soft cloth or by giving it a coat of shellac or varnish. As you gain experience you will find it easier to increase the complexity of your design. And, like the Slavic craftsmen have done, you may choose to display your eggs year-round as decorative ornaments or to present them as gifts.

3: The first wax (white) was applied and the egg dipped in red dye. Floral wax patterns were then applied over the red dye.

4: The second dye bath (blue) has covered the first (red) except in the areas where the wax resisted the blue dye. The first wax also resisted the blue dye and still preserves the white wax patterns.

This egg is decorated in the Ukrainian style called *Pysanka*. The mountainous Carpathian region is known for the elaborate geometric patterns such as this one; in the Ukrainian lowlands floral designs are popular.

An assortment of eggs in various stages of completion. The fine lines in the second, third, and fifth from the left, middle row; and the second from the right, top row, demonstrate what can be done by scratching through dye with a pin. A paint brush was used to "spot dye" the additional areas of color on these same eggs.

Geri Offerjost's art has evolved over the past 8 years from a kitchen table craft into a profession requiring a full-sized studio. She works on all kinds of eggs in a wide variety of styles, and owns a large collection of unusual braids and trimmings required for her work. She lives with her family in New Jersey, where she instructs classes on egg craft. She has exhibited widely, and gives frequent craft demonstrations.

Kitchen Celebrations
Imperial Easter Eggs

The Imperial Easter Eggs created by Carl Faberge in the 1880's for the Czar of Russia were actually cast from precious metals, inlaid with enameling and encrusted with jewels. Each "egg" usually commemorated an event like a royal anniversary or the Czarina's birthday and were presented as gifts throughout the year. The jeweler's exquisite craftsmanship coupled with his unique imagination produced art objects that are now treasured by private collectors and displayed in museums.

The egg form continues to inspire craftsmen who work in materials as diverse as porcelain, crystal, wood, clay, wax and, of course, chocolate and sugar. But the true eggers are those who perpetuate the tradition of working with the real thing. Though they work within the limits of a less exacting craftsmanship, their results can approach the jeweled appearance and inventiveness of the fabulous Faberge egg pictured on page 640.

Tools and Materials

Eggs decorated in the "Imperial" style can express your most elaborate, elegant, or outrageous ideas. Applique them with ribbons, beads, flowers and pictures, or make them into miniature, three-dimensional set pieces. Whatever your choice of theme, you will need the following materials: clean, unmarred eggs of any kind; water-soluble glue; pencils; watercolor paints and a paintbrush; paper towels; rubberbands (¼ inch wide); masking tape; a glass of water; a dish or container lid for holding small amounts of glue; and manicure scissors. Over the years, I have accumulated an extensive collection of "egger" paraphernalia—braids, ribbons, notions and costume jewelry materials. Undoubtedly, you will find materials of this kind around your own home, but you may have to make a trip to trimmings

Two completed eggs are decorated in the "Imperial" style with floral motifs. The pedestal egg on the left is finished with diamond dust, a glittery material.

and other craft shops before attempting to make eggs like those in the photograph on the opposite page. You will need plastic molded pearls; metallic braid or gimp; ribbon (not more than ¼ inch wide); a corsage pin; plastic pearl collars (in various sizes); jewelry findings such as stands and bead clasps; and a decorative print from virtually anywhere:(gift wrap, greeting cards, sugar packets or old fabrics). There are precut gummed papers, such as German Scrap, made especially for decorative applique purposes. For finishing you will need diamond dust, a transparent glitter that is available in several colors and grades at most craft shops.

Trimming and Finishing the Egg

Unlike *margutis* eggs, which do not need to be hard-boiled or blown, Imperial Easter eggs should be emptied before they are decorated. Follow the blowing method described on page 634. When the egg is completely emptied, rinsed and dried, you are ready to begin. By stretching a ¼-inch rubberband around the egg from top to bottom you can determine an even center line for the ribbon. Let the band lie flat and trace a pencil line along both edges (figure B), then remove the band. Pour a small amount of glue onto the dish or container lid and, with a toothpick, spread the glue between the marked lines. To wrap the ribbon, start at the bottom and pull tautly but carefully as you circumscribe the curved surface (figure C). Halfway around, stop and let the glue seep into the ribbon and mold itself to the egg. If there is any excess glue, wipe it off with a clean, damp paper towel. Join the two ends of the ribbon at the bottom and let dry.

Glue a pearl collar, small side down, to a stand. Set the egg on the stand, tilting it if you wish, and glue it down. To make the crown, stick a corsage pin through a bead clasp, a bead and a small pearl collar (wide end down on the egg) (figure D). Stick the pin through the ribbon on top of the egg. Cut a strip of molded pearls to be glued along each edge of the ribbon. Apply glue with a toothpick to the pearl strips by taping the strip, right side down, to your work surface. Also apply glue to the egg surface to be covered. Leave both until almost dry, then apply a second light coat of glue to either surface. Starting at the bottom, press the strip along the edge of the ribbon and cut at the top where it reaches the crown (figure E). Repeat for the three remaining sides. Using the same gluing method, lay the braid next to the pearls.

With a paint brush, spread glue on one surface of the egg and lay the print on it. Cut notches where the flat paper tends to buckle on the round egg (figure F), then press down the edges until smooth. When the print has dried, you can give

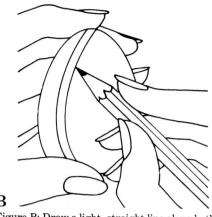

B

Figure B: Draw a light, straight line along both sides of the rubberband. Use a pencil; glue makes ink run.

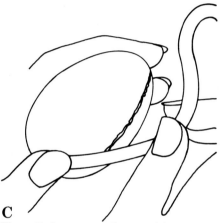

C

Figure C: As you wrap the egg with a ribbon, make sure you cover the blow holes at each end.

D

Figure D: An exploded view of the constructed egg shows how the corsage pin will pierce the ribbon and the hole in the top of the egg that was used to blow it.

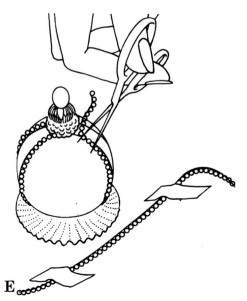

E

Figure E: The process of putting on the molded plastic pearls may be continued using additional rows of rickrack, gimp, or any kind of notion. Strung beads may also be used.

F

Figure F: Short straight lines on the paper design indicate where notches have been cut so the print will fit the egg's curvature without buckling when it is pasted down.

5: Pierce the eggshell with a manicure scissor point. Once the cutting gains momentum, do not stop to remove scissors.

6: During cutting, the contents of the egg keep the shell moist and prevent chips from flying. The wetness keeps the membrane attached to the shell, strengthening egg against breakage.

This picture egg was made from a speckled turkey egg. The items inside the egg were glued in, one piece at a time. The ground is dried moss, the fence a miniature plastic cast, and the bird is from a florist's shop.

The Renaissance Egg, worked by Faberge craftsmen and presented by Alexander III of Russia to his wife, is of milky agate set with mounts of gold, diamonds, and rubies. It is said that Carl Faberge kept a hammer expressly for the purpose of destroying any piece whose craftsmanship was not flawless.

the egg a porcelain-like finish by painting it with a mixture of glue thinned slightly with water. Or, while the glue is still wet, sprinkle diamond dust from a small pill bottle over the egg. Hold the egg over a container when you do this so the dust that falls off can be caught and reused. Tap the egg along the ribbon to shake off excess dust. At first the glue will make the print look milky, but the glue will dry and become translucent. Your egg is finished.

Eggs with an Added Dimension

Though ornamented in much the same way, cut eggs are decorated both inside and out. Choose an egg that is fresh and without cracks. With a pencil, draw the opening to be cut. With a small motor tool with a saw blade, the types of openings you can cut are almost unlimited. But a manicure scissors will do a good job if you you limit yourself to oval shapes and avoid sharp angles that might tend to break the shell. As you become adept at cutting, you will find that it is possible to cut more than one hole in the same egg.

Holding the egg over a bowl, pierce the shell with the tip of the manicure scissors and cut quickly along the pencil line with small shallow clips. When you have cut the entire opening, empty the egg into the bowl and rinse the inside of the shell. Never blow an egg if you intend to cut it, as blowing makes the shell brittle and susceptible to cracking. It is possible to trim the rough edges of the opening with the scissors, or file them with an emery board, but don't be too fussy as these will be covered by ribbon or braid. Decorate the outside of the egg following the procedures described above. Paint the inside of the shell in watercolor with a design or scene to create a setting. Place a figurine inside the egg, as I have done with the bird (left), and add finishing touches to complete your tableau. You will find that cut eggs are particularly adaptable to a variety of holiday motifs.

For related projects, see "Batik," and "Christmas Celebrations."